The Voice of Spirit Animals
from
'The Animal Psychic'

Jackie Weaver

Other books written by the author:

Animal Insight

Animal Talking Tales

Celebrity Pet Talking

ISBN 978-1500735012

1st September 2014

For My Darling Stan
Undying Love
2010 - 2013

Being able to pass messages on from deceased loved ones is something that mediums strive to do with compassion and honesty. Passing on messages from animals is something else entirely and yet, amazingly, that is what Jackie Weaver is able to do. She is a born animal psychic with an incredible gift, the gift of being able to communicate with animals.

She is a real life Dr Doolittle, able to connect with those that are still alive and wanting to let us know how they feel, and also those that have passed on to spirit. She gives absolute proof that they have survived the change that we call 'death', giving us peace of mind that they are happy and well. The animals give Jackie information that she could never have known unless they had told her themselves. Uncanny, but true!

In this book you will laugh and cry, as I did, at the heartfelt stories filled with emotion, joy and honesty, but essentially with the added ingredient of love and understanding which is the thread that runs throughout.

Jackie Dennison
Clairvoyant Medium & Host of
Rescue Mediums TV show

Table of Contents

Foreword – Introduction

I wasn't planning to write this book, but due to a tragedy, the death of my adorable cat Stan in 2013, this book, which was his idea, is written in his honour.

To take you back again to another year, 2005, that was nearly a tragedy too. I was diagnosed with non-Hodgkin's lymphoma (cancer of the immune system) and was stage four as it had spread to my liver, spleen and bones. I was extremely ill by the time they diagnosed me and only expected to survive a month at most! I spent my life saying, 'Every cloud has a silver lining' and through this illness I know I got more than just, 'a silver lining'; I became an Animal Communicator! This has changed my life forever, and I hope my work can do the same for so many others.

I know that Stan, who adorns this cover, chose me. He jumped up onto my lap whilst visiting a client (Sheenagh who is now a great friend) lay upside down long enough for us to take some photos (one of them you have just seen) and then I asked to buy him! He was about fifteen weeks old and the lady immediately said I could have him and so he came into my life. I can honestly say that I had no intention of getting a cat but do believe, if an animal is going to come into your life, it will! He was so cute and small, I almost christened him Dinky but actually named him Stanley after my own father, who lost his life to cancer when I was seventeen.

For three years Stan and I had the most wonderful time and he was the sweetest, funniest, cheekiest and most wise little boy ever! He was the subject of many of my animal communication courses and reveled in his fame on Facebook! On September 1st 2013, my heart was smashed into a thousand pieces as he was hit by a car and died instantly. Although I was doing spirit readings, I was numb with grief; totally inconsolable. Grief is an emotional and physical pain. I realised that we still have all this love welling up in our hearts that we shared with them everyday - it builds and builds and the pain of not being able to physically give it to them makes you feel like your heart will burst.

Over the years, I would class my readings as 75% 'living on Earth' animals, and 25% spirit animals. But, from the day Stan went to Heaven it reversed and has stayed that way to this day. For every spirit reading, I ask him to help bring forward the animal for their owner. Our connection is so special; it is beyond words.

I have written three other books, all true stories, but none solely on spirit reading stories. This book differs from the others as I have not written the stories myself this time; people have given me their story, in their words, about the communication I did for them and their passed over animal. It was Stan who suggested I do the book whilst chatting to another communicator for me. He suggested this idea of a format and I do hope you like it.

For anyone who has not experienced animal communication before (living or spirit) I will outline it briefly for you... Everything (animate or inanimate) is made of vibrating molecules of energy and energy is something that cannot be destroyed. Although we are 'alive' on Earth we are attached to our physical body that enables us to move around and live our life here. I believe that we come to Earth from Heaven (Heaven is my way of giving the spirit home a name) and we live here for as long as we are destined to do. I truly believe that we come in with a day set to leave/return. After all, with my illness I should not really be here but animals and people do sometimes seem to make 'miraculous' recoveries and stay longer than expected. As said to me by spirit dog from my *Celebrity Pet Talking* book, *'It is not Rest in Peace, it is Rest in Party, can you imagine the reunions that go on here?'* Take a moment to imagine it… You are now leaving Earth and your loved ones, who are already in Heaven, are watching and waiting for you to arrive to be with them once again. Does this not make you look at it in a whole new light?

When we connect to the energy/mind of an animal that has passed over, they communicate just the same as an animal on Earth and sometimes it is not obvious that they have passed over!

People send me a photograph of their animal and I work from that. I ask limited questions. Which are: the animal's name, gender, age when they passed and when. Technically I cannot explain how we can communicate with spirit, I just know that I, and thousands upon thousands of mediums and communicators, do it every day. Spirit know we can communicate on their behalf and sometimes they will 'jump in' and take over the reading that we are trying to do for an owner's other animal. They send us information via thoughts in the forms of: pictures, audio, physical feelings and a few other ways too. Also, sometimes we just have 'a knowing' of what they are trying to convey. Occasionally we give information that the owners cannot place at the time and even some that does come to fruition at a later date.

Whilst on a TV show, (I think it was ITV *This Morning*, although I have been on several and even a comedy show!) I was explaining my work and that some people grieve after their animals just like people do after the loss of a child. On a forum (filled with keyboard warriors) it was brought to my attention that people were very annoyed with my views and saying that it is nothing like that at all. Well, I stick to what I say and I hope that these stories will stand testament to that.

'Resting in Party'

Here is a dog whose presence in the saddest of circumstances was needed in more ways than one...

Lynne and her dog Hoochie

I first met Hoochie when my husband, Paul, and I were living and working in Turkey. Somehow, through fate, he was destined to be with me...

Paul and I had returned to the UK for Christmas having left our five-month-old white boxer, Buster, in kennels for that time. We returned to Turkey on New Year's Day 2000 and found to our disbelief that Buster had died on the day we returned. I was absolutely devastated and thought my heart was breaking. The kennel owner was also very upset about this, and he offered to give us his own dog, a tan coloured Boxer who was also five months old, called Hoochie.

I really wasn't sure, but my husband said yes straightaway. I have to admit it took a few days for me to bond with this poor dog. To be honest, he looked like a bag of bones and, bless him, trembled with fear in our car all the way home; but when I did let him into my heart, my God, did he become a mummy's boy!

My contract was due to end in Turkey and we had to return to the UK. There was no way on this earth that we were going to leave him behind, so I arranged for his flight, and at that time, he had to go into quarantine for six months. Hoochie flew home in October 2000, as my time in Turkey would end six months later in April 2001 - this way, we would be able to bring him to his forever home when we got back.

With Hoochie safely back in the UK, my husband Paul then had to fly home the next month due to ill health. Sadly, and unbelievably, he died soon after. So there was I, no Paul and no Hooch - I cannot describe the pain in my heart; my world seemed to have fallen apart.

I did manage to fly home and visit Hooch a few times, but it was heartbreaking having to leave him there when I left. He used to look at me with sad eyes, as if to say, "Why am I here? What have I done?"

I will never forget the day I went to pick him up. He wouldn't get into the car until he knew I was going with him. We had a great couple of months, but then Hoochie got hit by a car. I thought I had lost him too, but he pulled through, and although he lost one eye in the process, it never gave him a problem or affected his life.

As he got older, he had a few operations, as Boxers do tend to have back leg problems – but he just got on with it and was a complete star. He slowed down a lot during his last months; he was then thirteen years old. He used to sleep most of the time, and I had to coax him to even go out for a pee. He just didn't have the energy, and his back leg was giving him pain. He used to stand in the field watching the other dogs chase balls, and I am convinced he was thinking, "I used to do that."

I had to make the most difficult decision of my life when I had to think about putting him to sleep. Right up to the end, I didn't know if I was doing the right thing. But, decision made, my darling boy went to the Rainbow Bridge on 5th December 2012, the twelfth anniversary of my husband's death. It was now time for Paul to spend all those lost years with him. I was lost without him, and started reading a book of stories about how people coped with losing their pet, and kept reading about animal communicators. I was intrigued, and started researching it online. A lot of names came up, but I was drawn to Jackie Weaver for some reason. I contacted Jackie and arranged to have a reading over the telephone.

On the morning of the reading, I was nervous and excited at the same time, watching the clock and waiting. About ten minutes before my reading, the lights in my living room started flickering, which was a bit eerie, but then they stopped. Jackie rang me, and I felt so at ease with her. She started talking to Hoochie almost immediately. She told me things that nobody else could have known, and how special the bond was between us. I asked her how long before she rang me did she start to communicate with Hoochie. She told me ten minutes, which was the time my lights started flickering! I mentioned this to Jackie and she told me that as spirits are energy, they can do all sorts of things with electrics and that was him making his presence known.

Jackie told me so many things that made me laugh and cry, and everything that she said had meaning for me, which made me feel better about the dark place that I was in. Hoochie was such a character that you had to love him. When Hoochie said he was big and soft, but still a puppy, I replied that I always called him 'mummy's little puppy.'

Hoochie said his teeth were 'worn, not pretty, really not pretty.' I replied that this was something only Hooch and myself heard, I always used to tell him that his teeth weren't very pretty. Another thing that made me laugh, was when Hooch told Jackie, "The birds are just as loud here." I always used to complain about the noisy seagulls to Hooch, so lovely to know they make a noise in Heaven too!

Hoochie said that I was to stop crying and sitting on my own, there was no need. He also said, "You will never have another me, I was special." He said that I used to hug him, and he misses that and that he had had a fabulous life. He wanted to thank me for taking him, so, 'No more tears, you did a fantastic job, and I will always walk softly behind you.' He said he couldn't have felt more special, and he knows he will see me again.

When Jackie said to me that in Heaven Hoochie had found a lost puppy, I had to say to her that nothing registered with me about this. But, after the call I thought, 'Wow, he has found my Buster', the white Boxer who was a still puppy when he passed all those years ago in Turkey.

During my reading, Jackie told me that Hoochie had said that I had made the right decision, as he was in pain. He knew what a difficult decision I had to make and that I was very brave as I nearly couldn't go through with it. He also said that his passing was very serene, and he was walking much better now. I now look at the many pictures of him and know that one day, we will see each other once more, never again to be parted. I miss him every day, and now know I did the right thing.

I said that I would never have another dog after losing both my babes, but ten months later, I saw a ten year old Boxer girl that was being placed in kennels and thought there is no way I am going to let that happen! I know my boys would approve. There is nothing greater than looking into the eyes of a Boxer and seeing the love that they generate.

I thank you Jackie for the wonderful reading and for connecting me with my loved one. I now truly know that every animal who will share my life here on Earth will eventually go and live with Paul until it is my time to join them too.

R.I.P. Hoochie, my darling little boy xx

*****

A 'gem' of a dog...

Joanne and her dog Gemma

Gemma was my beautiful Tri-colour Collie girl that I got from a rescue kennel when she was nine months of age. She was: gentle, loving, loyal, funny, and a true member of my family. She suffered a stroke when she was thirteen, and then slowly slid into old age before passing in my arms at home at the age of fifteen.

I felt I couldn't get over losing Gemma so, although I had never heard of animal communication before, I turned to the internet for help and found Jackie. We arranged a time and date and Jackie rang me at the allotted time and explained animal communication to me, and how we would have a three-way conversation with Gemma.

Jackie started by giving her impressions of Gemma – she was a sweetie-pie, happy-go-lucky, and with a lovely nature. This was all spot on; she was such an easy going girl and for the first time in weeks, I felt as though Gemma was close by again.

Jackie went on to say how Gemma used to sit by the side of the settee when I was watching TV – this was true; she was such great company. Gemma told her that her paws were often wet, but would dry quick!

That made me laugh. (Living in a rural, and often muddy area, when the dogs came back from a walk we would dry their feet with a towel before they came into the house.)

Jackie then said she got the impression that Gemma's mammary glands look bigger. I was quite astonished by this. Gemma had a lipoma (a soft fatty lump) on her underside that made one side of her chest look bigger than the other.

I smiled when she told me Gemma was aware that she was a fit looking dog when she was younger and was a, 'hey, look at me' dog! I told Jackie this is probably because I was always telling her how beautiful she was!

Gemma then showed Jackie a stone in the garden that seemed to be heart shaped. I must admit, I couldn't immediately place this but then I realised the connection. Not long after we after we had buried Gemma, I had placed a stone on top of her grave - it wasn't a memorial stone, just a little stone I spotted on the path that was a natural heart shape. It is so nice to know she's seen that. It was also wonderful to know that she had seen me pick up the photo of her from my bedside to talk to her.

I was feeling a little sad at this point in the chat, so Gemma took the opportunity to tell Jackie how she used to burp! Very ladylike, but that is exactly what she did! She'd usually wait until I bent down to kiss her and then she would burp in my face and make me laugh! Even from spirit she was still making me laugh.

Gemma told Jackie that I couldn't decide on a name for her when we first got her. This was true; I tried a few different names to see if she responded to any, and then finally settled on Gemma. I asked Jackie if she liked the name, and Gemma said most certainly did because she was my "little Gem." That's just what I used to say to her!

One of the main reasons I asked for Jackie to communicate with Gemma for me, was because I worried we'd let her go on for too long I needed to know if she had been in pain, or I that had let her suffer in any way. Gemma reassured us that we didn't let her suffer, and we had nursed her and made sure she had everything she needed. I felt reassured by hearing this, and was able to let go of some of the guilt I'd been carrying around since she had passed.

I felt lighter and happier after the spirit chat – although I still miss Gemma so badly, I felt as though she was closer to me again, and not gone forever.

Thank you Jackie x

*****

A lovely horse who eventually let the music play on…

Lisa and her horse Tig

I was really pleased when Jackie asked if I, and my Tigger, would like to feature in her new book and I'm sure my Tig (as we affectionately called him) will be quite proud too! Writing our story is going to be incredibly difficult as, although it has been seven months since my boy became my spirit horse, my feelings are still raw and I miss him so much. Anyway here goes through the tears…

It had always been my dream to have my own horse, and even at the age of three I made everyone refer to me as Jessie James (the cowboy) and apparently wouldn't acknowledge anyone if they called me by my real name. In September 2007 my husband, Jimmy, and I were lucky enough to find our dream home with six acres and four stables and in March 2008 I got my first horse! His name was Tigger (Royalview Replica), and he was a stunning chestnut Anglo Arab, eleven years old. I fell in love with those sweet, honey brown eyes right away…. I was hooked.

The first couple of years proved rather challenging with my boy as he was an extremely intelligent chap and was always ten steps ahead of me! I did some research into his history and found out I was about his seventh owner! His previous owners were much more experienced than me but he obviously proved too much for most of them and after being thrown off him a couple of times he had been sold on. Although I did have a few falls, the first one being within my first few weeks of owning him (leaving me unable to ride for six weeks), selling him on was not an option. Despite me not being hugely knowledgeable of 'problem' horses, I was committed to this boy and would do whatever it took to gain his respect. I did not want to go down the route where I was using a whip and spurs on him etc., and it wouldn't have worked anyway. He had obviously had that kind of treatment in the past and was definitely not going to put up with it anymore.

The turning point came in about 2010 when I decided to do lots of ground-work and see what happened. Tig was a very quick learner and we both got pretty good at it and eventually we would work in the arena together at liberty (without headcollar etc.). Tig's favourite trick was to go stand in the arena on his pedestal (a wooden ramp) with his lips pursed waiting to give me a kiss so he could get his treat; or as soon as he got into the arena, he would start side passing down the fence... anything for a treat! He had such a sense of humour and used to make me laugh every day.

We eventually had such an amazing relationship, a great bond and a deep understanding, respect and love for each other. Tig and I spent lots of time together and he was the centre of my world, and we knew each other so well; which is why on that awful day, I immediately knew my boy was not quite right.

It was a nice day in July 2013 and, as usual, I put him out in the paddock in the morning with his two elderly companion rescue ponies (Poppy and Hermione) who absolutely adored him. I am lucky enough to be able to see the paddocks through my kitchen window and I noticed Tig was just standing by his paddock gate calling me. The ponies seemed to be acting a bit odd too. I told my husband I was going to bring him in as he didn't seem right.

I went down to him and he gave me his usual deep, loving neigh as if to say 'Hi mum.' I walked him up to his stable and settled him down. He didn't even go to his haynet, which was very unusual... I called the vet immediately. Whilst waiting for the vet, Tig stood resting his head on my chest whilst I kissed his handsome, noble face. In the meantime my friend, who was there at the time, brought the ponies in as I thought he would be happier with them nearby. I am so lucky to have a great equine vet practice twenty minutes down the road and, thankfully, the vet turned up within half an hour.

As soon as she turned up he lay down, and I began to get a horrible feeling deep in my stomach. My heart sank. I knew something was very wrong. We got him up again so the vet could examine him. After a thorough examination she said he was probably a bit colicky so gave him an injection of painkiller. Within minutes I noticed my boy's legs start to tremble which I pointed out to the vet. The next thing I knew Tig appeared to be having some kind of violent fit. The vet dragged me out of the stable and rang for assistance. I could not believe what I was seeing and kept shouting repeatedly, 'Oh my God! I can't believe this! What's happening?' I was so lucky to have such an understanding vet and she tried to comfort me as best she could whilst we waited for the other vets to arrive, but I could tell by the look on her face she had never seen anything like this before.

After what seemed an eternity but, in reality, was about a couple of minutes, my boy fell to the floor and was still conscious. He was breathing really heavy. I was distraught. I begged the vet to let me go in with him, which she did, but made it clear that if he tried to get up I was to get out of his stable immediately. She couldn't believe how - as soon as I lay down by his side and started talking to him gently, telling him everything would be okay - his breathing calmed right down. I lay next to him kissing his face and gently stroking him. It's so difficult even seven months down the line to remember the love of my life just lying there.

Within about twenty minutes another three vets turned up (one of whom was one of the top surgeons from the practice). They put Tig on a drip and sent off bloods - of which the results came back within half an hour... but they showed nothing. After about an hour of him being down Poppy (his companion) started literally throwing herself around the stable and acting very oddly. This was even more distressing as she was very old and had several fairly worrying conditions herself. No one could believe what was happening. My husband, Jimmy, and my friend were in with her whilst the vet tried to sedate her. It was awful. I was trying to keep Tig calm as he could obviously hear her, and her him.

After two hours of tests the vets were still unsure what was wrong and could only put it down to something toxic they had eaten due to both Tig and Poppy being very ill. About two and a half hours had passed and I lay next to my boy absolutely heartbroken…. I couldn't let him suffer anymore. I turned to one of the vets and said "I don't want my boy to suffer, you understand what I'm saying don't you?" He put his hand on my shoulder and said he did and I was doing the right thing. The vet came into his stable and hugged me and reassured me I was doing the right thing … we both cried.

I hugged and kissed my Tig and with great sadness watched the light go out in his beautiful, intelligent, deep brown eyes. I was inconsolable and broken hearted. I had held it together until this point as I wanted to remain calm for Tig. I remember repeating over and over I couldn't live without him. My whole body was shaking…. I was in deep shock especially as I also had to get Poppy put to sleep literally a couple of minutes after Tig as she had got to crisis point too and was simply too old to cope. I stayed with Tig for a couple of hours afterwards until both him and Poppy were due to be picked up. I kissed him for the last time and said goodbye. It was unbearable. I was dead inside. My wonderful Tig had such a big personality. The place felt empty. I was lost.

I am lucky to have a very understanding husband and family, but no one could console me. The vets were assuming it was a toxic issue and it was just terrible waiting for the post mortem results. Time just seemed to stand still.

A couple of months before my Tig went to spirit, my cousin contacted me and told me about a brilliant book she had been reading written by Jackie Weaver. Needless to say, I bought the book and thought it would be great to have a reading with her so I could have a chat with Tig to see what he had to say - which was probably a lot. However, on several occasions when I tried to contact Jackie via e-mail, my laptop crashed so I tried to text her and, for some reason, my text message wouldn't go through either. Somehow, I just never got round to contacting her after that until Tig had passed, although it was always my intention to have a reading with my boy, I just never imagined it would be a spirit reading.

A few days had passed without my Tig and I was in an awful state. I needed to speak to him to see if he was okay. This time when I tried to contact Jackie, my email got through and my reading was arranged.

The day arrived when I was due to speak to Jackie. My cousin came over to offer me some moral support. I decided to have the reading in Tig's lorry surrounded by all his photos. So, with my cousin beside me, we sat there nervously waiting for Jackie's call. I was extremely nervous and emotional as it had only been a week since I had lost Tig but I had no reason to worry as she made me feel very at ease. The reading with Jackie absolutely blew my mind.

At the start of the reading I knew immediately that Jackie had connected with my boy by what he was telling her, things that no one else could have known, like silly things we used to do. I was in no doubt that Tig was there in spirit talking to us... I couldn't believe it.

What really blew my mind is what he told Jackie about the day he and Poppy passed over. She gently said she thought there had been three hours trauma before he passed over, and that he said he had no blood in his gut – i.e. his and Poppy's deaths were not due to toxic poisoning - which Jackie wasn't aware that they might have been. He said he felt an 'explosion' in his head and he didn't feel right – Jackie suggested it sounded like a bleed or burst in his brain. He told Jackie word for word what I was saying when he was having his seizure. He even told her that when he fell his head was in the corner of the stable (which it was as the vet and I were trying to make him more comfortable and move his head).

Since Tig passed over the radio in the stables had broken.... Well, I say broken - I just couldn't get any station on it, just a buzz. I asked Jimmy if he could fix it for me as I always had the radio on in the stables. He said for some reason it didn't have a signal so I just switched it off with the intention of buying another one. Which is why when Jackie asked me was I having problems with the radio my heart skipped a beat. "Yes!!!" I said. She then went on to tell me that it was Tig's way of letting me know he was there. She told me that now he had got his message across that I should go and try the radio again. At the end of our phone call I thanked Jackie, through my tears, for the most wonderful reading and, needless to say, I dashed to the stables and turned the radio on. Sure enough, it was working fine, on its usual station and the song playing was UB40's *I got you Babe*. I was absolutely over the moon that my wonderful horse had actually tried to let me know he was with me in spirit through the radio.

I remember at the end of the reading he said, 'Tell my mum thanks for sending me off with lovely feet.' It was only a few days before he passed over Tig had his feet trimmed, as was the case every six weeks, and his feet were looking great and I actually commented to the farrier how great his feet were looking. Bless him.

About ten days after speaking to Jackie and Tig, I had a call from the vet regarding the post mortem results. She told me that Tig had had a blood clot on his brain and suffered a stroke! I was stunned and immediately sent a text to Jackie saying what a clever boy Tig was as he knew that and was able to tell us. Poppy's post mortem had not revealed anything in particular (no toxins) and they thought that as she was so old the trauma was all too much for her. Tig was right!

Although I was obviously still heartbroken, and still am at losing my soul mate, having that reading with Jackie has made things bearable and changed how I feel spiritually. Knowing that Tig lives on in spirit and is happy and knowing that he loved his life here with me helped me carry on. I can't imagine how much worse I would be feeling now had I not had the chance to speak to him. Having the opportunity to speak to him was priceless and I will be forever grateful to Jackie for that and for helping me through my grief.

*****

One little dog who wanted to talk about everyone and even convert the family sceptics...

Mary and her dog Buddy

Our darling Buddy came into our lives in a rather dramatic way ten and a half years ago. I was on the south side of Dublin city walking along when I became aware of this beautiful large, blond and white dog wandering and looking lost and distressed.

I watched him for a while and realised that he was trying to latch on to people, mainly men. Instinctively I went to him and petted him and he seemed more than happy to be in my female company too. There was an elderly man sitting in a car waiting for his grandchildren to come out of school and he too was watching the lost dog. We exchanged a few words about him and I just mentioned that I would have taken him home myself, only I was travelling by bus. "I'll drive you home when the children come out of school," he offered, and that was it.

After a bit of 'gentle' persuasion, my husband took our new guy on board, and this beautiful dog joined our family. It took a while to find the right name for him but I think Buddy was a great choice because that is what he became - our Buddy.

We already had two cats, Sid and Nancy. Sid (now also deceased) was a very laid back and a tolerant fella – he accepted our new dog without any problem. Nancy was another story! She has a mean streak!

Buddy could best be described as a total gentleman. He was so affectionate, kind and loyal. He was a sensitive soul and hated to hear any type of argument or loud voices. He was also incredibly handsome and I was so proud when people stopped me on the street to ask what breed he was. He was, of course, a mixed breed but people just adored him. I walked him every night and a few people would stop and admire him every time. 'He is stunning' was the usual compliment. Buddy just loved his walks - he was ready every morning for his walk to the park or the beach with my husband, Danny, and come the evening time, he would watch me closely until I reached for his lead. As a young dog he was full of life and energy and would race around the beach or park.

In the last year of his life Buddy had slowed down considerably, although there were times when he would slow right down but then would pick up and be himself again. Eventually, for his sake, we had to scale back the length of his walks.

I have to admit he was very spoilt and extremely fussy about his food. My husband Danny cooked chicken and rice for him most days as Buddy turned his nose up at dried or tinned food! Why not when you can have chicken and rice! There were a few visits to the vets, mainly for his medicine for his arthritis and he was well in himself, so we were completely unprepared for his very sudden departure.

On Thursday 17th October, Buddy had been slow by the end of his short morning walk but appeared to be okay all afternoon, just relaxing in his bed. That evening I discovered, to my horror, that he could not stand. I was on my own in the house and could not lift him up to take him around the corner to the vets. Panic set in. I rang my cousin who lives nearby and he came round immediately. He had difficultly lifting poor Buddy too so he ran out to the garden and came back with a wheelbarrow. It wasn't easy getting him into the wheelbarrow either, but we did and wheeled him round to the vet.

It was near closing time and the female vet examined Buddy briefly. She said she could not diagnose what was actually wrong at this point and said she'd give him an injection to make him comfortable and would run blood tests in the morning. I left my darling there and that is the last time I saw him alive. I got a call from the vet early the next morning to say that Buddy had passed away in the early hours. Quietly and without fuss, that was our Buddy - but what a shock!

Four months on and we were still devastated. Our daily routine was no longer the same and we remembered all the mornings and evenings we spent with him. There is a huge space in the sitting room where Buddy slept on his bed, where I tucked him in every night and said good night to him. He could never be replaced. There will never be another like him.

He was so terribly missed (and still is every day) which is why I had decided to arrange a reading with Jackie a while after he passed away. My husband and daughter thought I had 'lost it' and, to be honest, found the whole concept rather amusing and unbelievable.

I arranged a time with Jackie and I was a little bit apprehensive. I need not have worried; she was so nice and put me at ease straight away. It was very consoling to get in touch with Buddy and I have to say that I was stunned by the accuracy of some of the information and also information regarding other pets in the family.

Jackie in her reading also described Buddy as a gentleman, just as I always did! She talked about our first meeting and that he was lost and looking after himself at that time. She also gave a name, which she thought might be a road name relevant to where he came from. I checked up on this and there is a road name in that same area! Incredible. More incredibly, Jackie asked if we had a cat in the family with a "saggy" belly. She had just described our Nance! A fourteen-year-old female cat with a distended tummy! Admittedly, Nance is also totally spoilt and Buddy described her in the reading as 'the one who gets to do everything she wants.' How observant of him! Jackie also mentioned a white cat. I couldn't place that one at the time but later it dawned on me - I had a 'visitor' here for a few months before I found her a home and she was mostly white.

Jackie also asked about a little black boy dog that seemed to be a little sausage type who Buddy described as a 'little bugger'. That was our Pigger who had passed away nearly two years previously. He was also found as a stray – adorable but with a real stubborn streak and very streetwise. When talking about Pigger, Jackie said the name 'Rory' kept coming up and did I know why or recognise it. Amazing – in his previous life I had discovered though the grapevine Pigger was actually called Rory.

Jackie said Buddy was showing her a Reverend or Priest – I recognised this straight away as Buddy had been to the blessing of animals in our local church only about ten days before he left us – how touching that he was recalling this to us. He went on to tell us that he just became a very old man and had pressure inside but he is free from all discomfort now and had passed away peacefully without pain or suffering. It was very consoling to hear that. He also expressed gratitude for his life with us and for taking him in. Heartbreaking! We were the lucky ones to have found him and to have had him for ten and a half years.

I have to say my sceptical husband and daughter could not believe the details of Jackie's reading when I relayed them. I was gloating, needless to say! Thanks Buddy! We still miss him but we will all meet again 'over the rainbow' and that goes for us, Nance and any other strays that find their way into our hearts too.

*****

Timing is timing, and this boy's call was booked and he was coming through, whatever…

Anna and her horse Blarney

Blarney was a very handsome 15.3 coloured cob type, full of character, cheeky and loving and definitely had a sense of humour. I bought him when he was nine years old from a friend. I knew his history from when he was about a three-year-old but decided to have a five stage vetting anyway. He passed with flying colours and the vet said he was extremely fit and healthy. I couldn't quite believe I was so lucky to own a horse like him!

He was perfect for me - sparky enough, but really safe and jumped anything like a stag at speed. We hacked for hours on our own and competed at a low level. We won a Riding Club National Show Jumping Competition in Lincoln as part of the Shrewsbury District Riding Club Team which amazing but, after that, things went downhill.

To cut a very long story of many years short, Blarney had episodes of looking, and being, seemingly unwell. We explored absolutely every avenue to get to the bottom of it - he was up and down with many different symptoms that came and then just went. I even took him to a Vet School to get thoroughly examined but they couldn't find anything wrong with him either.

A couple of people suggested animal communication to me and, although I had an open mind about it, it never quite got to the top of my list. When I eventually did email Jackie to find out how to go about having a communication with Blarney, ironically, it turned out to be his last couple of weeks, aged only fourteen. At this point in time, he seemed totally fine in himself and I had actually got round posting my letter to Jackie along with his photo etc. as I kept seeing articles on what she does and people were talking about her - it was as if someone looking over me was desperately trying to get me to get in touch with her! She emailed me my appointment and I was intrigued as to what my boy would say.

One evening the livery yard contacted me to say he hadn't eaten his tea and had started to look a little unwell. I didn't want to take any chances so decided to get the vet out. Usually, if Blarney had antibiotics, he would come right again back to his normal happy self. On the way to the yard to meet the vet, I had this awful feeling that something devastating was going to happen and I was right.

It was a new vet who came out to see Blarney and gave him an intravenous (into the vein) injection of antibiotics. Blarney started struggling to breathe almost immediately and it seemed as if there was nothing that could have been done to help - he died about 15 minutes later of anaphylactic shock. The conclusion was that he had had an allergic reaction to the antibiotics. I have to say, this was the most horrendous thing that I have ever experienced and I was distraught.

The next day I was so devastated and heartbroken and didn't know what to do with myself. At 12 o'clock my mobile rang. I answered it and it was Jackie ready to do my communication. I was so upset and told her that it was too late now; my Blarney had died last night. She tried to console me and said that although it was very soon after his passing, if I wanted to continue, she would carry on for me as it might help. I agreed to go ahead. My heart was pounding at the thought that I might be able to communicate to him after this terrible ending but felt it was probably too good to be true.

Jackie described his personality to a tee and then said she was experiencing shortness of breath which she felt Blarney had been feeling as he died. I hadn't told her any of the details, but she started telling me about how he had been ill on and off for a long time with breathing problems and stomach pains, which all rang true. I believed what she was saying but the cynical side of me was trying to question it. Then she said, "He wants to thank you for pulling him up on the stubble field the other day." She told me I was with other horses having a canter and unusually, he couldn't keep up with them, so I stopped him. He said he felt like his legs were going to give way. 'Oh my God!' I thought, 'This woman can talk to animals!' That was exactly what happened a week or so before! He pointed out that, although the way he went was such a shock and not particularly pleasant, it could have been much worse.

He gave us a sad scenario to imagine if one day he had collapsed whilst out on a ride and suffered some terrible painful injury to either himself or me, then having a long wait for help etc. etc. it wouldn't bear thinking about and would have been even worse than actually what did happen. As difficult as that was for Jackie to pass to me, it did make sense and he was right.

She said physically it seemed like there was some unusual area up near his chest that would not have been very apparent but, for some reason, would periodically flare up. We will never know what actually was wrong with him but he assured me that, on the whole, he felt fine and loved his riding. Jackie said that Blarney knew he had a post mortem and not to worry because that was just his body, not his spirit. He felt brilliant now and was more handsome than ever and his white bits were extremely white!

She said, 'You know how when you used to take him to competitions he would be calling and whinnying to everyone as you walked through the lorry park?' (Which was so true, he was hilarious saying hello to everybody he saw.) 'Well, that is how he arrived to the other side.' This was heart warming to hear.

Blarney also used to back into me all the time trying to get me to scratch his bottom. Jackie said, "He's worried about how he's going to get his backside scratched now!" Very apt and typical Blarney! There were so many things that were so spot on and couldn't be guessed, it was fantastic. Above all, it was that he hadn't felt well for a long time and he was now healthy and happy. If I wanted to talk to him, just to speak out loud, or from my mind, because he could hear me.

This reading, at such a crucial time, really helped me get through his passing - it would have been a million times worse without it. Heaven has certainly gained another Angel and a handsome and cheeky one at that. Gone, but never forgotten.

*****

A little girl who, I think, would describe her life as 'A piece of cake'...

Fiona and her dog Misty

Misty was a black miniature poodle and such a big character for a small dog but, even bigger than her character, was her heart. She and I met when her first owner moved into sheltered accommodation and she had to go to an adoption centre. She was already ten years old and had quite a few health issues but I wanted her regardless - so she came to live with me.

She adapted to her change in circumstances remarkably well and, once her health problems were under control, she quickly made it clear that, in her opinion, she was the brains in the household. She was probably right! Having Misty and Chloe was such a joy. In time, two youngsters that also needed homes added to our family unit and life was bliss.

Misty seemed to know a great many things in advance; she knew when a visitor was coming, even when I had no idea, and would wait in the hall for them to arrive, and the amazing thing was, she was always right! She was absolutely charming to anybody she met. She was immensely polite and she loved people.

In the park she would notice if there was a person sitting alone on a bench. She would wander over to them and just sit down and look up at them to see if they would like some company. She would wait until they noticed her and said hello and, if not, she would meander back to me. If she met a child who wanted to pet her, I could trust her completely. The most clumsy pats, strokes and prods were received equally graciously as though she were thinking, 'How lovely, another new human to love!'

She was not into exercise, she preferred reclining on the sofa but she came for walks just the same. As she got older and not so well, she liked me to tuck her into my jacket and carry her. I would put her down in nice grassy spots and she would have a sniff, and do whatever she needed to, then ask to be carried to the next place. Since she was a small girl this worked for everybody. The younger dogs got their walks and Misty did not get left out. We kept this up until the day before the day she died. She was a complete darling.

Many of Misty's stories involved food. Food was her specialist subject which I was soon to find out shortly after her arrival. My other poodle never looked in shopping bags so one day, when I tossed a couple in the car with the girls, I did not think twice. It was only a five minute drive back home but, in that five minutes, Misty had found the packet of mince, unwrapped it and eaten the lot! Lesson learned! Misty was one of those girls who struggle with their waistline. Well, she didn't struggle with it, I did. She did not approve of diets although she was on one more often than not. All it took was a split second and to spot a shopping bag and, if I didn't make it across the room in time, something would go missing from the bag and end up inside her! She was clever and very slick with it! No wonder she had a weight problem!

We had six wonderful years together and, when her health began to fail, my vet gently suggested that it might be kinder to think about putting her to sleep. I know he was doing his job and trying to be kind, but I decided just to take it one day at a time and trust that I was not being selfish as I truly felt she was not ready to go just yet. She was weak but able to eat and drink and let me know when she wanted to be carried out to the garden. She was not unhappy and still would make me smile with her little gentle loving ways.

She spent a lot of time looking at me very calmly, but intently, and in the last few days and I would gently ask her if she wanted me to take her to the vet. I followed my instinct but on her last morning, I asked the same question, and she never took her eyes away from mine and I just knew in my heart, it was time. I felt like somebody a great deal wiser than I am was looking at me. When she died she did it with such gentleness, it was like a leaf falling off a tree. She took a breath, breathed out and was gone.

At first, I felt that I had done what she wanted but then I started to worry that I had got it all wrong and just kept her alive because I could not face taking her to the vet. I began to really torture myself about it. That added to my grief at missing her badly was a very painful combination. That was when I started searching for an animal communicator, and I found Jackie.

The reading with Jackie was astonishing in the accuracy of the details about what Misty had liked and disliked in her life and various ailments she had. Also, when Jackie spoke Misty's words for her, I could feel her bold character shining through just as it had when she was here with me. This made me feel confident that she really was communicating with my beloved girl. She told me how caring Misty was, whether that was people or dogs – she just loved everyone and life. It was beautiful to hear that she understood why she had gone to the adoption centre, taken it in her stride, and appreciated how lucky she was to have had two loving homes.

It was heart warming when Jackie talked about many details of her passing. She described how I had carried Misty out into the sunshine in the garden when I thought she wanted to be outside, and that the birds had seemed very loud in their singing - I had noticed that too at the time, so had Misty it seems.

Jackie described the way that Misty had stared into my eyes for the last few hours of her life. Misty said that she was very glad that I had followed mine, and her feelings, and let her go when the time was right. This was the hugest relief to me. That morning I had told Misty that if she wanted to go, then please don't try and hold on just for me. She did, in fact die, a few minutes after I had whispered that to her.

This is not everything that Jackie told me and I still smile when I think that, even when connecting from spirit, food still seemed high on her agenda – so lovely to know that my efforts were appreciated even though I did my best to disguise the, 'you're on a diet but we won't mention it'. Misty laughed with us about my various efforts to try and fool her! Anyone who has another dog in the house that needs different feeding requirements will know how tricky this can be. Boy, they can make us feel so guilty!

I do know the vets also remember her so fondly as Misty had more than her fair share of vet visits for her Cushing's disease and certainly became a real favourite with the nurses. It only took her a single visit to discover that they sold particularly delicious chews there and establish her vet-visiting routine. We would go in, then Misty would march up to the receptionist's desk and ask for her chew. She knew I would always buy her a treat for being a good girl, which she always was. It would be put aside for after the visit. Having seen the vet, she would then collect it and march purposefully to the exit, with an air of, 'Thank you very much, see you soon!' That always got a giggle.

There were so many other details that meant something only to Misty and I but I hope it is enough for people to know that this is real and that Jackie is not just a lovely lady with a big heart but also a really brilliant communicator too.

I will always miss Misty's cuddles, but I now know that she goes on and that sometimes she is here even if I cannot see her. I can never thank Jackie enough for that.

*****

A dog who communicated to her owner from the spirit world and then guided her to me...

Helen and her dog Holly

A diamond is special, one of a kind, and as the song goes, 'A girl's best friend!' My dog Holly was just this to me. She was a medium sized, short coated, black and tan mongrel from the RSPCA - two years old and needing a loving home. The day my husband

and I got her, I felt so happy I was tearful. I was overjoyed to be taking her home but desperately hoping her sweet eight-week-old puppies she was leaving behind, would not be there for long either.

We had Holly for eleven memorable, happy, contented years, receiving all the love we could ever give as she gave to us unconditionally too. She shared our life, our holidays, simply everything with us.

As time went on, old age crept up and things really started to trouble her. Eventually we made the heartbreaking decision to have her put to sleep. We knew we had to release her from the discomfort and while she still had some dignity left. We knew it was the right thing to do, as hard as it was. The vet came to our home, we said our goodbyes and she passed away peacefully. She had an individual cremation at a quiet, tranquil place in the Cumbrian countryside - but the morning after, I woke up tearful thinking of her when, suddenly, a voice came inside my head and said simply, "I'm okay." I was so surprised 'hearing' this but from that moment on, I knew there really was a spirit world - it was such a comfort to me and made coping with her passing so much more bearable.

A few months later I felt the need to contact an animal communicator. It was as if I was 'guided' to pick Jackie as this had to be a special person to do a spirit reading for our girl. I felt quite nervous, apprehensive and slightly sceptical prior to Jackie calling me.

When I got the call, Jackie told me various things and then asked if Holly had a kink in her tail? She did! From that moment on I just knew it was Holly on the 'other side', as it were! Holly talked about how lucky she felt as she was never separated from us in the house and how she remembered being let off the lead the day we got her – she was so overjoyed and just full of affection for us, her new family. This was all so true and amazing!

Jackie talked about Holly's stomach problem and the medication she had for this. Holly assured me that the time was right when we let her pass over to the spirit world. One of my most heartfelt moments was when Holly said she remembered how I would so tenderly cup my hands around her head and ears and then kiss her on her head.

Jackie told me that she could see Holly sitting on what looked like wooden decking simply enjoying watching the world go by - this made me smile as it was the balcony at our lovely little static caravan in the Lake District where she'd go and stand sniffing the sea breeze and relishing the sunshine! So many beautiful memories were made there. Holly said that there were many times she would be curled up on her bed and we would be talking about her. She would look as though she was asleep but, every now and then, would open her eyes as she really had been listening to what we were saying. We always thought she understood a lot, but little did we know how much!

Jackie asked if I had any questions for Holly myself. I did and it was to ask if she ever comes (visits) my bedroom? Holly said yes and has even left a gentle paw dent on my duvet. I had asked this question because... I have a sensor light on the floor in my bedroom and, for no apparent reason, it has been coming on when nothing has been moving. Sometimes it even happens during the night, and I feel it is Holly coming into my room to just be with me. It fills me with joy to know that even though she is now a spirit animal, she can still come and visit and even jump on our bed.

After this communication, which I wanted to go on forever, I felt amazed and uplifted but naturally still sad that I could not cuddle her physically anymore. Then, as the days passed by, things that Jackie told me from Holly would come into my thoughts and make me smile. Thank you for this wonderful connection, our heartfelt thanks go out to you from Holly and I.

*****

An Angel of a cat who was sent to Joan to undo heartache from thirty two years ago...

Joan and her cat Bobby

I had been feeding a black short-haired cat, as a stray, for about two years. I decided to call him Bobby, and over time, he gained trust in me. I would always find him sitting on the back doorstep waiting patiently but he would never come into the house. Even when the door was wide open with food belonging to my other three cats clearly visible, he would not enter, so I put food outside for him.

One day I suspected that Bobby was having problems with his teeth because he cried out when he was eating. I managed to coax him into a cat carrier, and took him to the vets. The vet ended up removing some of Bobby's teeth and we took this opportunity to have him neutered too. Because it was wintertime, and freezing cold, I needed to keep Bobby indoors while he recovered from his operations. Bobby was crying and wailing and became very stressed. Having made sure my three cats were inside the house, and the cat flap locked, I took Bobby into my bedroom for the night. Bobby eventually settled down and went to sleep and made my house his home from that day on!

My other cats (Rollo, Jake and Amber) never welcomed Bobby, although they never ganged up on him or attacked him - they stayed together and didn't try to befriend him. As Bobby really loved attention from people this did not seem a problem for him anyway.

Not long after Bobby moved in, I went away on holiday for a week that I had booked a while ago and had organised my neighbour to come in three times daily to feed the cats. Unfortunately, because of my being away, Bobby became stressed and after a few days my neighbour told me that Bobby had taken himself off only returning briefly to eat via the cat flap, then leave again. When I returned from my holiday, Bobby came in for some food but when he saw me, he ran away. I was so upset for him, and me. The next day when Bobby came in for food I shut the cat flap so I was able to keep him in. Once again I was then able to cuddle and talk to him but, as soon as the cat flap was open, Bobby took off again. After a couple of days of love and coaxing, Bobby settled down and happily stayed with me again.

After this situation, I always took him to a cattery so he would get attention and cuddles. This was easy because Bobby was so loving, so vocal, a real chatterbox. He was so friendly; everyone that met him loved him. When people called at the house, Bobby would come running up to them, just like a dog would! He would come and ask people for cuddles himself; he would sit in peoples' arms like a baby with his front legs around their neck. If Bobby could not find us he would cry, and, on many occasions, I had to get out of bed to show Bobby where I was!

He always ran to meet my son, Philip, when he heard his car pull up and he would jump inside the car for a cuddle. He often watched us eating and liked to try any foods regardless of what they were - he tried spicy sausage, various cheeses and many other human foods.

Bobby went out one night in January, probably to stretch his legs, patrol the area and use the toilet. Sadly, he did not come back to us alive and it seems he did then, as he often did, chased other cats out of the garden and across the road. This happened just fourteen months after he moved in with me and my son - to say we were devastated by his passing is an understatement. At that time, I had been retired for about eighteen months and Bobby helped to fill my days. Don't get me wrong, my other cats are lovely, but they are very independent and are not into cuddles etc. They do sleep on my bed but do not snuggle up into me like Bobby did.

Because I was struggling to come to terms with losing Bobby, my son Philip looked up on the internet for a pet psychic and found a lady who claimed she could talk to the animals in the spirit world. So we sent a photo of Bobby along with the fee. We waited patiently but heard nothing and eventually discovered that she had gone to Australia for a month! With still no email response to ours, we gave up waiting and my son went back on the internet and found Jackie Weaver. He wrote explaining that they had been let down and again he sent a photo and fee. Jackie expressed her sorrow that someone could have been so thoughtless and unprofessional at such a time of grief, and sent us a date when she could phone, which was within two weeks of contacting her.

When Jackie called me, I felt like I was talking to an old friend - she is a lovely lady and definitely had connected with Bobby. She was amazing in her detail and explained why Bobby had become so stressed when we left him that time. Having had a loving relationship in a household for the first few years of his life, his owners had moved away and he ended up having to fend for himself as a stray. (Jackie seemed to think he had been given to someone in the locality but kept returning to his original home that was no longer his, so ended up homeless.) When he found me, and eventually moved in, he was so happy but when we went away for that week, he thought I too had moved away and left him behind once again. This explained so much and I am so glad I had then always sent him to a cattery after that. We would leave him there and he would get lots of attention but knew we would always come back for him to bring him home.

Jackie told me that Bobby's death was so fast that he didn't even remember being hit by a car - he went out like a light. My vet had already stated that it must have been very quick. Jackie described the location of the street where Bobby passed over and confirmed our initial thought; it was because he was chasing other cats. She told us how much he loved us and gave us other information that could only be relevant to us.

I was most amazed by the fact that I have homed more than a dozen cats some who lived to be fifteen and sixteen but she told me that Bobby was with another cat called Blackie and asked if I knew a Blackie. I didn't know how she had picked that name out from all the other cats names she could have chosen but, I actually had had, not one, but two cats with that name! I asked Jackie if she could ask which Blackie it was and she told me it was a cat I had had 32 years ago. I told Jackie I knew who she was talking about. Jackie said she felt there was some sadness about the situation as if things had not been straight forward and was being told to tell me to please let go of any guilt.

I then told Jackie that the 32 years ago was exact (that year is etched into my mind) and the incident she was referring to was when I had taken Blackie to the vets to be put to sleep at the age of eight. She had a chronic life long illness that I was unable to pay for at that time in my life - things were bleak to say the least. I had no insurance - I was desperate. I tried everything and when I asked the RSPCA for assistance in re-homing her, I was turned down because they stated that it would be too difficult to re-home a cat of that age with medical problems. I ran out of options, and as much as it broke my heart, I had Blackie put to sleep. I have carried that guilt for 32 years, but my Bobby had brought Blackie along to tell me that she understood that I did, what I did, because of love for her and did not want me to feel guilty any longer.

Jackie said she could hear the name 'David' and asked if that meant anything to me. It certainly did. That was name of my stillborn son also from that sad year, 32 years ago - I lost him not just him, but Blackie too. So all these years later, thanks to Bobby, who really was the most precious of cats, even in spirit he brought me such precious information and the release of a long carried burden of guilt. Thank you my boy.

My son had been a little sceptical but could not believe what Jackie was telling me - I want to state that Jackie did not try to gain information from me or get any clues and what was said just seemed to roll off her tongue and it felt like when someone is reading a book. During my lifetime, things did improve and no stray cat that walked into my garden has gone unfed, or gone without medical treatment. I have a very good vet who is used to me bringing in waifs and strays and I just pay for the medication. Most of the cats that I have owned have adopted me! In fact, I have only chosen five myself and I have to say the stray cats have been the most loving.

My thanks go to Jackie for her help, she has helped me more than I first realised. It has still taken a little more time to come to terms with the loss of Bobby and Jackie did say that she thought Bobby was going to send another cat my way. I was hoping this would not be the case because losing them is getting harder to deal with. However, this thought was quickly disregarded when, in walked Oscar, a nine-month-old black male cat the image of my little Blackie, the one who died 32 years ago! He also loves cuddles and jumping into my son's car! My son said he is like Bobby in many ways, but not quite!

Thank you Bobby, and, although losing you broke my heart, from Heaven you helped heal it too. You really are one in a million.

*****

Who would have thought, whilst on a train journey to do a TV show it would lead to this reading...

Lisa and her dog Douglas.

I, and my ex-partner, had Douglas from twelve weeks old. I had always wanted a Basset Hound since childhood, so it was a dream come true. Bassetts are defined as 'stubborn' but more that they will do what they want to do - and when they want to do it! Saying that, everyone who met him loved him, and my mum adored him too. He was stunningly handsome and would always turn heads wherever we took him. Douglas was always my baby and I treated him like that.

Two years later we decided to get another Basset although something was telling me not to get another one; however, we did, and before long we lived to regret it. The new boy, Jeffrey, as we named him, attacked Douglas and not just once, it happened time and time again. We tried many ways to try and work it out but to no avail and sadly had to rehome Jeffrey. He went to a loving older couple where I believe he had a happy life but struggled with his health.

Unfortunately, during the period of upset caused by Jeffrey's behaviour, Douglas developed bouts of colitis. We had to feed him only scrambled egg and rice until his tummy settled back down, which it always did. He also developed a mental condition about drinking water; once starting to drink, he just didn't stop! He would just go into this 'zone' so when we thought he had had enough, we had to tap him and then he would stop. We also discovered he had developed a heart murmur but luckily this showed no signs of affecting him and he didn't need medication.

He lived a very happy life despite the occasional colitis blips.

When Douglas was seven, my ex walked out on us, then two weeks after that, my Dad lost his year-long fight with cancer, and went to Heaven. I was losing everything, including being made redundant three months later - my life seemed to be falling apart at the seams. Douglas was my life and he gave me the will to keep going, to get up in the mornings; after all, I had him to look after, and I wasn't going to let him down. He healed me with such unconditional love; he really was my life and wherever I went, he went. He ate when I ate and slept when I slept. I talked to him all the time and knew exactly what he was thinking and was sure he understood my every word. Life eventually got better and my mum looked after Douglas whilst I was at work.

On Thursday, March 15th, as I pulled up onto my drive, I just knew something was wrong. I went in and found mum was on the floor with Douglas as he had just collapsed a few minutes before I got home. I rushed him to the vets and they told me it was serious and they would need to x-ray him to see what was going on inside. It was really busy that evening, so I sat on the theatre floor with Douglas waiting for the vets to come and get him.

Unfortunately the x-ray confirmed the worst - he had internal bleeding as his spleen had ruptured. They told me that they could try to operate on him but they didn't know what else they would find when they opened him up. I begged them to save him, try anything - he was my life. At one point, I think they thought they would succeed in saving him but as they were finishing off doing his stitches, his heart gave out and he passed over. I was devastated and saw him one more time for my last cuddle. He looked so peaceful - just like he did whilst asleep on the sofa at home.

I had to have a week off work; I just couldn't stop crying - I had never felt so alone. I had always kept in touch with his breeder and called him to tell him the news and he asked me to go over to see him. When I got there we talked, cried and laughed about the good times. He also showed me the puppies that were nearly ready for homing, I just couldn't look at them - nothing would replace my Douglas. We went for a walk outside and a beautiful seven-year-old Basset Griffon named Jodi was out in the paddock. She was lovely, so pretty and gentle, we had a play with her and then I left.

When I got home I had realised that I had left my jacket there so had to go back the next weekend to get it back. Jodi was in the paddock again so I went to see her and the breeder said if I wanted her I could have her! She had been a show dog once but didn't get on very well showing so needed re-homing. In fact, she had only been to three shows and just lived in the kennels with all the other dogs. The breeder said she might struggle to settle into home life, as kennel life was all she knew, but I could take her on a four week trial and see how it went.

That was the hardest four weeks of my life. Jodi was scared stiff of everything: she didn't know what carpet was, ran down the garden and wouldn't come in for hours, when the microwave dinged, you name it, she was scared to death of it. Even going out on a walk was nerve-wracking for her but I was consistent with her. We would just literally go around the short walk three times a day for weeks until she got used to it then extended the distances and places and eventually she got used to things. Since then she has come on amazingly well.

A while after this, my friend Sue told me about this person she met on a train called Jackie and that she, although in front of others, had chatted to her pet there and then! Sue bought me a session with Jackie as a present and I duly sent Jackie a picture of Jodi and arranged to speak via Skype. During Jackie's communication with Jodi an amazing thing happened – Douglas butted in and made his wonderful presence felt again!

Anyway, after we had done Jodi's reading, Jackie promised to call me that evening to continue with Douglas's. I was nervous / excited all rolled into one as I had felt so guilty about his passing and hoped he was okay about me getting Jodi. I took notes and the following is what Jackie said and what Douglas told Jackie (both in italics to make it easier to understand) - followed by my comments.

He tells me he was your pride and joy, where you went he went. 'I am soft and cuddly. If my mum told me to fetch a certain toy I knew which one to fetch.'

So true, he was so switched on and did understand me!

Did he have chest problems, a rattly chest? I said I understood this.

He says, 'I was so brave, I just went to sleep, it was like the candle was snuffed out.' Did you have him put to sleep? I told Jackie that I didn't but his heart gave way at the end of an operation, so he didn't wake up.

He says you weren't expecting it, as it seemed he had not been a poorly dog. He was a brave boy and this took the decision out of your hands. He said he was

Jackie Weaver

utterly spoilt. 'I was like your child.' Everyone said how spoilt he was. True!

He would just sit and watch you doing things; he was always with you. Why is he giving me a strong smell of food, and food cooking? We laughed as I explained he was a food monster and could be fast asleep but, if you got something to eat, he was by your feet in seconds! We had to keep an eye on his weight and titbits were really not supposed to be allowed.

He is now showing me a plate of scrambled eggs! Ah, that was his colitis saviour. We had a giggle when Jackie told me as a child she hated them as they always seemed to be like rubber, and come to think of it, they always were weren't they?!

He says when you were in a rush to go somewhere, you would take him out to do his 'business' but would be repeatedly saying, "Come on. Douglas. Hurry up. We have to go." This, it seems, made him drag his feet even more! I laughed. *I am sure he knew what he was doing!* Oh yes, I totally agree. It is as if he knew that I was in a rush because he would go even slower, sniffing everything and delaying me. Stubborn or what? I remember one day when it had been snowing, we were walking back across the road and he sat down in the middle of the road and wouldn't move, and I mean, would not budge! Cars had to stop until I could move him - well, when he decided to give in, that is. He made everyone laugh.

He is now showing me him trying to get under, or going along under, a hedge, like he is trying to hide from something. How funny, yes, the rain - he hated it! He would do anything to try not to get his feet wet. Once we were out and we walked over the fields, over a bridge then round. When we got to the stream again, this time there wasn't a bridge. Quick as a flash, he ran back in the direction we had come, then appeared at the top of the field, crossed that bridge and ran back down to me again. What made this more amazing was that we had never been there before. The lengths he would go to not to get wet and dirty, apart from fox poo that is! If he could find some of that, he would roll and roll and roll in it. Gosh, why do they find it just so utterly delightful?!

Having listened to me telling Jackie about his 'reverse round trip' Douglas cheekily mentioned the other option which would have been to lift him over the stream. She stopped abruptly and asked, *'Why is he showing me 5? He wouldn't be 5 stone, would he? So you couldn't have lifted him anyway!'* Yes 5 - he was 5.5 stone!

He says it was always your dream to have a Basset Hound. He was a very personable dog, very human.' How wonderful he knew he fulfilled my dreams.

He is holding his ears up, and maybe rather smelly ears at that? Oh, bless him; he used to hide when he knew you wanted to do them. *He says he was grateful as he could hear better once they were done.* Strange happening at this point…my Skype sound totally went and Jackie's end went really loud! It was just like he was showing us the comparison of before and after. After that, the sound went back to normal!

Why am I seeing lots of water being sucked up and spilling? I explained his odd water drinking issue.

He says he wasn't stressed just needy. 'I was like a single child, I just wanted to be with you.' He just lapped up the affection. He is asking, 'Was it a problem?' I quickly replied, "No definitely not,

Douglas, I loved you." How extraordinary that we could have this three-way conversation; it felt so wonderful to be able to share memories, thoughts and assurances with him.

'He says you brought the best out in each other. I don't usually get into personal things like this but did he fill a gap for you with a relationship break-up or something like that?' Yes, he most certainly did!

He is laughing saying he became the man of the house. He also says you used to ask him questions like: "Where should we go today Douglas? Where would you like to go for walkies? What shall we do today?" So true!

Were there some 'oddities' going on inside around his pancreas or something up in that chest area? (That is where the spleen is situated.) Douglas butted in with, *'She could have hugged me forever but it wouldn't have changed anything - there was nothing she could have done, I had internal bleeding.'*

He says, 'I fulfilled my life, I had an amazing life, I went over peacefully. As hard as it was for you; it was easier than you having to make the decision.' I then explained to Jackie about his spleen and the operation to try and save him.

Was there someone else in the household, as it seemed to be more than just you? Yes, mum used to come in and look after him when I had to go into the office.

Douglas says, 'Nana spoilt me too. When my 'mum' wasn't there, she would say, "Here you are son, have a biscuit."' He is laughing and saying 'You caught her handing me one once - it was so funny!' One of us had try to be strict with his weight!

Do you want to ask him anything? I braved it and asked her for his feeling about Jodi, my present dog I got after his passing.

Douglas says Jodi loves the rain. He is laughing, saying he is horrified as she splashes around and gets all dirty. 'Oh my goodness, what a mess! She is like a whizz-machine she runs all over the place.' He was really pleased you got her as you have a lot of love to give. He goes on to say, 'I want my mum to be happy; I had everything I could have, absolutely everything. I was her treasure.'

Douglas says pictures adorn my house, note, MY house! He is laughing and saying, 'You didn't think you would hear from me again! I am perfect and I am fine. Think of me when I was four. I think I looked at my best then!!'

He is fading back now, and tells me he going off to stick his nose in something he shouldn't.' So true of him! *He is glad he fulfilled your dreams.*

I asked, "Who he is with? " *He is with a man who was weak at the end, and seemed like he was shaky.* This is my own dad; his 'Gan-gan'.

I am not sure if this is right, as names are not my strong point, but is the man called Jeffrey? "No", I replied, "but I do know who Jeffery is." I quickly explained the story of Jeffrey and why we re-homed him and knew that he had passed over.

Douglas is now back with Jeffrey, but they are now absolutely fine together. He says, 'We had to live our own lives' and is laughing as he says 'but I will always be the better looking one!' He blows you a kiss and says,' I love you, Mum'

I have thought that I have heard Douglas before but have always wondered why, as we were so close, I never feel, smell or see him. I always wondered if he really was on the other side. I wanted to say sorry for me not being with him when he passed over and have prayed that he was not scared he was frightened in the operating theatre. Jackie has confirmed he went really gently which has eased my guilt - I know my boy is safe in Heaven. I couldn't believe when she mentioned Jeffrey, very few people knew about Jeffrey, they always just remembered I had Douglas. I am so happy that he has made up with him, but the best laugh was when he said that he was still the better looking! Sorry, Jeffrey, but he was!

The reading has now confirmed to me that animals do go to spirit. It was always something I thought, as I couldn't believe my boy just no longer existed in this universe. This reading has given me great comfort beyond words. It was also so lovely to know he knew I had Jodi and what she is like and that he wanted me to share my love. I always did believe that the Angels took me to her, and now know it to be true and I am sure my darling boy had something to do with it as well.

How wonderful that a meeting of two complete strangers on a train could bring me such personal happiness in the way of a spirit animal communication.

*****

*This amazing dog managed to breach the divide
between science and talking to spirit…*

David and his dog Shadow

My Eulogy for Shadow…

*He was my friend, companion, anchor and teacher. He was
my saviour, as I was his. He was the one true constant
during a time of uncertainty. He offered me his heart and I
gently took it with both hands. It was the start of a bond
that has stood the test of time and has only ever grown
stronger. I never had to look for him because he was always
by my side. He entwined himself into my heart and soul to
the point where it was impossible to say where he ended and
I began - a relationship that remains impossible to unravel.*

*He was that rarest of creatures, a once in a lifetime dog
whose very existence centred solely around me, just as mine,
centred solely around him. Each day was an adventure. It
didn't matter where we went or what we did just so long as
we did it together. We were never apart and shared every
day, every experience together.*

*He fell asleep taking a part of me with him, a part that will
only be returned once life has come full circle and we can
start a new journey together. He will wait for me as I would
him but until then, we will be together in dreams.*

He was my rock, he was my brother, he was My Shadow.

The first time I saw Shadow I was instantly drawn to
him. He was a big specimen of a German Shepherd
Dog, proud and strong and I estimated his age as
being around two-years-old. The first word that
sprang instantly to mind was magnificent, and it was
a word I heard repeated often from people seeing him
for the first time.

Let me explain how this meeting occurred. I'm a
professional Canine Behaviourist and I was visiting a

security dog training kennels in a professional capacity. Shadow had just returned to kennels following deployment and marked down for further training as apparently he had a bit of a reputation as being 'difficult'. In reality, and as I discovered, he was just misunderstood. I spent as much time as I could with Shadow, taking him out of kennels (which he hated being in) where we would just sit together in the sun whilst I groomed and talked to him. His big brown eyes would fix me with a stare, and his head would tilt first to one side then the other - it was as if he was desperately trying to understand what it was I was saying to him. When I left the kennels a few day's later I was really sad to have to say goodbye.

A week later I received a phone call from Shadow's owner saying his dog was due back to his kennels having bitten someone on his new guarding job. He informed me that the dog's future was now very bleak, in fact, his future was being measured in days. Before I knew it, I had blurted down the phone, 'I'll have him.' I'm not sure who was more surprised me, or this kennel owner! I already had two dogs at home and was not ever considering adding a third. In my heart, I knew I couldn't let anything happen to Shadow, so I jumped in the car and drove very quickly (one might say the speed limit may have been broken a couple of times) back to the kennels.

Shadow recognised me immediately and was just as pleased to see me, as I was him. The kennel owner and I started discussing Shadow's future. The phrase PTS (put to sleep) was repeated several times until he suggested a price to save Shadow from the fate he had planned for him. Talk about blackmail. Anyhow, I wrote a cheque, bundled Shadow into the back of the car and drove home with him vowing never to go back to those kennels again, and I never did!

That was the start of nine years together where we were inseparable. Everywhere I went, so did Shadow. He became a very well travelled dog, working with me, with other dogs, and seemingly taking everything in his stride. Life though has a habit of throwing things at you, sometimes not pleasant and sometimes very hard but, throughout my hard times, Shadow was always by my side. Later on, I met Helen, and she too fell in love with Shadow - life was good.

Fast forward to April 2014. Shadow had just finished his dinner (he loved his food) and was sitting in the lounge, panting. As I looked at him I noticed his abdomen was distended and knew it was not from the food he had just eaten. I felt his stomach area and it moved like there was fluid in there. I immediately phoned our vets. After describing what I had felt to the vet, amongst his words, 'possibility of cancer' hit me hard. After arranging to take Shadow to the vets first thing the following morning, I couldn't believe what I had just heard, as Shadow was as he always was: full of energy, eating for England and beating up our young Border Collie. It took me some time to take on board that Shadow was no longer a young dog and the nine years we spent together, seemed like no time at all. I realised he was not indestructible; he was fallible to illness just like the rest of us.

The next day the vet said that he could feel a mass on Shadow's spleen. He explained to me that the fluid in his abdomen was actually blood following an internal bleed. He thought it was a splenic hemangiosarcoma (cancer of the blood vessels) and that the only option was to operate to remove the spleen and mass. We were warned however, that should there be evidence that the cancer had spread to his liver or elsewhere, then the kindest thing would be to have Shadow put to sleep on the operating table, there and then. It was made clear, if they did not do surgery, he would be dead in a matter of days. It felt as if my whole world had just collapsed around me and as I looked at Shadow as he busily sniffed around the car park without a care in the world, the realisation hit me that my 'big lad' wasn't going to be with me for much longer. My heart was breaking into a thousand pieces. The last thing I wanted was for Shadow to 'go' on the operating table so Helen and I, insisted they ran a battery of tests to see if there was evidence of the cancer spreading and, once we had those results we could make the decision to operate or not.

The next day we were back at the vets for Shadow to be x-rayed and bloods to be done, and Helen and I hung around there waiting to hear the results. When the vet appeared to say there seemed to be no evidence of the cancer anywhere else, we breathed a collective sigh of relief and gave the go ahead for the operation.

Shadow came home that evening looking a bit groggy but, even after a massive operation, was still able to polish off his dinner in record time as well our collie Dexter's left-overs! The vets had recommended we have a biopsy done on the growth they had removed and over the next few days, whilst waiting for the results, we fell back into normality. Shadow recovered quickly although he had developed a slight limp in his left hind leg but it didn't seem to bother him, and it certainly didn't slow him down. Then came the phone call from the vets confirming that the mass was indeed malignant and, in spite of being operated on and previous test results, this was an aggressive type of cancer so nothing more, other than palliative care, could be offered. He was given six to eight weeks but this was an optimistic time frame. Once again my world fell apart.

Shadow carried on with his life as if nothing was wrong whilst I set about planning his funeral, a task that took on an almost surreal aspect, especially given that Shadow appeared, well, just Shadow. Then on the Sunday night before he died, Shadow was struggling with his left hind leg - the cancer was spreading. I phoned the emergency vets and we took him for an examination. The one thing about many dogs is that they are past masters at covering up whatever ails them and Shadow was no exception to this. From hobbling around on three legs he suddenly transformed into his old self, aware of everything around him and ready for action. He was prescribed something for the pain and off we went.

On Monday he was only slightly better but the medication he was given upset his tummy so it was back to the vets on the Tuesday for a change of medication. Wednesday morning there was a transformation in him for the better. He was most insistent to go out, barking and getting excited and half ran, half stumbled, to the van afraid we were going to leave him behind. I helped lift him in and Helen, Dexter, Shadow and I, set off for the bluebell woods as they were a favourite of his. He was just like a puppy: keen to investigate every blade of grass, rolling on his back, loving the moment and soaking up the warm sunshine. When we got home, Shadow contentedly settled himself down in his favourite position in front of the sofa where I always sat, and soon he was snoring for England. It was when he awoke I noticed the difference - he was struggling with his left leg and obviously uncomfortable. Shadow began to 'distance' himself from me and I had this terrible feeling in the pit of my stomach. He lay down by the patio door and just stared at me as if he was trying to imprint me on his memory.

Helen woke me at 5am the next morning telling me that Shadow couldn't get up. I ran to him and we helped him into the garden so he could at least go to the toilet. He looked defeated and he just wouldn't take his eyes off me – the time had come. I knew I had to make that phone call and the vet arrived at 11.30am. Shadow, once again, demonstrated his resilience to pain but it didn't last long and he settled down looking tired. A sedative was given and he slowly relaxed, laying down next to me. My hand rested on his heart as the amber liquid was injected into him. I felt his heart slow and then stop as Shadow let out a final sigh. He was gone and I was alone.

The days that followed were dark and miserable even though the sun shone. Nothing felt right anymore and I just could not shake the feeling that I was no longer whole.

I was sitting at the computer one day when, all of a sudden, 'pet psychic' came into my head. Now, as I have previously mentioned, I am a professional Canine Behaviourist, trained and tutored in science and very sceptical of anything relating to the paranormal. However, I did a Google search, and up popped Jackie who I then remembered seeing on TV once before.

I read with interest what she had to say and I checked the testimonials on her website. I then went onto

Amazon, downloaded her free book and when Helen came home, I told what I had been up too. Helen was very supportive, so I sent Jackie an email and following a telephone conversation, a date had been set for a reading. I freely admit saying to Helen, that nobody knew Shadow as I did and it would be very clear in a very short time whether this was all hocus pocus or not.

Come the time of the reading Jackie was her bright and friendly self whilst I, on the other hand, was a complete nervous wreck. As the reading progressed, the only way I can describe it was akin to a beam of sunlight shining through the darkness of a stormy sky. I was talking with MY Shadow of that there was no doubt - unless of course Jackie had Shadow and I followed for the past nine years! Through Jackie we reminisced, we laughed, we cried whilst all the time the feeling of emptiness began to recede.

Jackie described in detail the medical condition Shadow had and the moment of his passing. Unless Jackie had been in the room, there was no way she could have known what transpired other than being told by Shadow.

Shadow's attitude to his cancer was that nothing had caused it - it was just 'sods law', which is a much used phrase of mine and one he had obviously heard me say countless times.

Shadow went on to say about his obedience and especially his 'stays'. Shadow's obedience was second to none, especially when asked to stay. Whenever we did any work, at the end of the exercises Shadow would always come galloping up to me proud as punch with a big, soppy grin on his face as if to say, 'I did it, Dad.'

At one point Shadow showed Jackie a cliff's edge. This made her panic a little with the vision of a dog and cliffs, which actually gave Shadow and I a bit of a giggle. Helen, Shadow and I, had been on a visit to my sister who lives near Buxton. I had taken Helen and Shadow to Stanage Edge where I use to climb the cliffs. Shadow also mentioned our other holiday in Cornwall. Those two places were actually the only proper holidays we had due to work commitments. I have some wonderful photos of those times and after the reading, I had the strength to dig them out. Happy memories.

Shadow said that I 'think like a dog' which, being a canine behaviourist, I took as a huge compliment as its meaning was I could also see things from a dog's point of view too. I couldn't help but laugh at his next comment when he said that coming to work with me was easy, especially when he didn't have to do anything! True!

Shadow said that before our lives together he wasn't cared for, not abused, but definitely not wanted. He said about being passed from pillar to post when he had been in the kennels and that they could not force the aggression out of him. Everything being relayed back to me through Jackie resonated to the point where it was like hearing the past nine years being read back to me.

I have to say, one of funniest things was when Shadow commented about my website. He told me exactly the same thing that Helen had; that my website needed more pictures because so much text was boring! I never thought for one moment I would be taking website advice from a dog and it will be changed in his honour.

There were so many intimate details of our lives together, details that only Shadow and I would ever have known and yet, Jackie relayed them to me one after another.

The overwhelming feeling I had throughout this reading was one of such love, especially when Shadow said he missed his hugs just as much as I did - we were big huggers Shadow and I, more often than not initiated by Shadow, but always willingly returned by me.

After the reading I sat and cried like I have never cried before. It was a combination of missing Shadow but also one of relief. It was just so comforting to know that I was not alone anymore and that Shadow would always be with me, and that I had done right by him and, him by me. As Shadow said, 'It hurts so much but it was worth it.' I couldn't agree more. I always knew that if I gave my heart it would be broken but, give it I must for it was all Shadow asked for in return.

Since the reading I 'feel' Shadow with me and for that, I have Jackie to thank. Jackie, you have opened my eyes and my heart and for that I shall be eternally grateful and, as Shadow so pointedly said, 'Love is not science.'

Thank you.

*****

A little boy who, from Heaven, inspired and guided his owner to do more on her spiritual path...

Neshla and her cat Fred

Bubbles my cat, fell pregnant soon after her first litter of kittens were born so we didn't get a chance to have her spayed before she gave birth to yet another four beautiful black kittens. The first time round, it was easy to find a home for the kittens, but this time we had more trouble finding a home for them! We had already kept one kitten from the previous litter and had decided that it was only fair to keep one from this litter too. However, we only managed to find good homes for two of them this time (although I must admit we didn't have much time to try too hard). We named them Fred and Barney as my kids were huge Flintstones fans and our previous cats had been Pebbles and Bam Bam.

Sadly Barney got run over when he was only a year old and Bubbles passed away not long after that although we never really knew the cause of her death, she just died peacefully in my arms. Fred therefore was on his own and he certainly enjoyed being the one having all the attention! He was an extremely friendly cat and would not let anybody walk by without first stroking him as he would manoeuvre in front of their feet until they had at least given him a stroke! Fred was spoilt, he was like an only child enjoying all the attention. A friend, who was not a cat lover, said she couldn't help but adore him as he was such a character. When we used to have friends round he would literally jump on one lap and flop himself down for a while, before getting up and draping himself over the next person. He never curled up like most cats – he would dangle over people or things! He was so loveable and had the softest fur imaginable. I work from home and he used to position himself in my in-tray so I couldn't get to my paperwork – or would push it all on the floor so I had to get down there and sort it out! Whilst I was down there on my hands and knees, he would sit there watching me with a twinkle in his eye and I am sure a wry smile on his face!

Sadly, one day Fred decided to chase a bird (one of his favourite pastimes) but while he was concentrating on catching the bird, he went straight onto the main road where was hit by an oncoming car. My son's friend happened to be behind that car (which heartlessly just drove off) and saw Fred there lying injured on the ground still with a the bird between his teeth. He brought Fred over to us but I looked into his eyes and could see he was not going to be with us for very long. We took him to the vets and held him gently whilst he was put to sleep.

I phoned Jackie as she has previously helped with my animals and had spoken to Fred before. When she said she would ask him what happened, he showed her an image of a cartoon cat with stars going round his head! This was so apt considering how we choose his name. Fred said he was dazed and didn't know what was going on but he did make me smile saying that the bird had gone to Heaven with him too! He showed Jackie him jumping from a wall - I knew exactly what she was talking about as unfortunately on the other side is the road where he was hit by the car and a route which he normally avoided. He said he was reunited with the other cats and had already done his job here on Earth although he was only three years old. I have to say, for one so young, I always felt there was something extra special about him - it was a feeling that you couldn't really put into words if asked.

Jackie made me laugh when she told me she could see sheets flapping about and couldn't work out what he was showing her. I certainly knew - Fred was a pain when I tried to make beds as he would get under the covers while I was trying to do this. With a fitted sheet, I would be doing one corner and he would go under and pull it up and when I got to the final corner, I would notice a lump in the middle and see Fred has sneaked back in! He would then try and catch the duvet cover when I flapped it straight before putting the duvet inside and given half a chance would dive inside it too! He was such an adorable monkey, so typical of him. Bed making will never be the same without him but due to his antics, even now the chore of changing the beds brings back sweet memories. However, I have to admit, at the time I was always frustrated doing this chore as it took me double the effort but bless him, he has certainly made sure he will never be forgotten.

Fred told Jackie that he has met up with his mum, Bubbles, and through Fred, she said she wanted to thank me for looking after her and also for keeping some of her kittens. I thought that was really lovely.

Fred went on to tell me that he had fun playing with my lights in the bedroom! This was so true as they were always switching on and off seemingly on their own accord. He also commented that I would be surprised on what else he could do in spirit. Following that comment, he went on to talk about the psychic work that I was doing and said that I would be branching out to do many more things than I was doing at that time and was only doing a small bit compared to what I was capable of. He said he could see me standing in front of a crowd of people talking to them, and low and behold, he was right! I now teach many different types of classes and now even organise my own psychic fairs. I would never have believed how quickly the spiritual side of my life would develop and I know that he is watching me from afar, and I know he is proud of the work I do. I also find that when I do readings and have trouble putting things into words for someone, I mentally ask Fred to help and do you know what, he does! Although losing a loved one (person or animal) is never easy, at least we know there is an afterlife and we will be re-united when the time comes.

Fred said he was happy where he was and we shouldn't worry about him. He also told me he loved it when I used to call him "my best boy" although he was the only boy in the house! He said was proud of Pickle (our cat from rescue) since she was settling in well after having such a bad start to life. (He had spent some time with her before his passing and was very sweet and welcoming to her when she arrived. She was not quite the same to him, or us, as she was very untrusting but, in time, and with some help via Jackie and her communication skills, she has blossomed into a relaxed and loving cat.)

Although I miss Fred and of course my other cats too, I know by having had a reading with Jackie that he is happy in Heaven and playing around just like he always did. Out of all the cats I have had, he is the one that seemed most human and had such a character and it is so good to know he is safe and well. Thank you Jackie for all of your help as this is not the first time you have reassured me that my pets are safe and happy.

*****

A Christmas Angel complete with halo...

Sophie and her Cat Snowy

'What would you like for Christmas?' My husband asked. I did not hesitate for a moment... A friend for our resident boy cat of six months!

I hastily made a call to a work colleague who was friends with a truly wonderful lady who ran a rescue home in her own house and garden. So, in spite of our wintery weather, my gorgeous boy arrived by train to London Victoria station carried by my friend. He then spent Christmas Eve in the office with both of us before heading home by car for another hour of travelling. As I watched my new little boy, so comfortable, whilst the snowflakes dotted the windows, I decided to christen him Snowy. Once home, it was straight off to the vets for a check up and treatment for an eye infection. It wasn't serious, or contagious to our other cat, so it was home at last.

I was expecting him to be nervous, exhausted, or disorientated at the very least, but not so. This small, rather round, little bundle of white and black fur, was just happy to be in our home. He settled instantly. He loved our existing cat and played happily with the Christmas decorations for the rest of the evening! That night just after I went to bed, he jumped up on the bed, curled up, and slept in the crook of my arm. This was his preferred place of slumber for many years to come!

I was smitten! I instantly felt a deep bond and connection with this lovely gentle bundle of joy - he just stole my heart!

For five happy years we shared our home with our boys! Snowy made friends with a stray cat that had appeared. He even shared his food and his favourite spots in the garden with the poor soul.

Then, tragedy struck; our dear cat Prince was run over. We were deeply saddened and felt it was our fault as we had recently moved house. He had been my husband's cat and was a handsome confident boy - we were heartbroken! Poor Snowy was clearly missing him. He was withdrawn, quiet, hiding himself away, not playing and not his usual happy self. Such a sad time!

We then adopted a kitten who sadly was also run over just eighteen months later. Just terrible. To compound this sadness, my cat of 20 years also passed over. He had retired to my parents' home some years ago as I used to take him for visits and it became clear he would rather stay where they lived. I dearly loved him but decided his happiness was more important so let him live out his senior years there.

A few days later sensing my sadness, Snowy jumped up next to me and looked up to me as if to say, 'We still have each other!' He never left my side and over the next 6 years we were inseparable; he was a joy, fun, lovely, gentle and full of character! He seemed to remain young and kitten like; he was my baby! There are not enough adjectives to describe what a gentle and joyful soul he was, even non cat lovers took to him sensing his delightful character. Every cat in the neighbourhood visited and the local birds used to eat from his bowl!!

His annual visits to the vets were uneventful, thankfully and although he remained a little chubby, he was happy and well! Then one day I noticed he was a bit off colour. This went on for a couple of days and was unlike him, as he had never been ill. I thought it would pass and maybe he had a tummy bug or suchlike. Despite thinking about a visit to the vet, I did not take him, as he was not ill, just not quite himself.

Thinking back now, I can't forgive myself for not doing so, it was almost like I loved him too much to accept he may be unwell - it could not happen to us! Then one terrible day my husband and I noticed him in the garden unsteady on his feet, clearly unwell and in pain. I was truly devastated. He was admitted to the animal hospital and spent three days in intensive care. The vets were kind and said at best he had a chance of surviving a few months but the prognosis was poor. He was diagnosed with a serious heart condition, thyroid and kidney problems! This was so unbelievable as he had been so well, displaying his usual kitten like way just a few days before! I visited and stayed with him almost the whole time he was there. He would only eat when I was there and it was clear to me he needed to be home.

Also, unbelievably, the day after my boy was admitted to the vets, I was told I needed urgent surgery too and, on top of that, my husband was suffering from an ailment and had to go into hospital as well! My little family was in turmoil! I was also having a challenging time at work but oddly enough this led me to be able to work from home full time for most part of the next year. Fortunately this meant I could care for my boys without the pressure of working away!

Snowy rallied round and for the next eleven months I nursed him at home. I attended to all his needs, gave him his tablets and injections, and stayed with him as much as I could. All my social life was organised around being with Snowy and tending to his needs. I was up every night to check on him and up early each and every morning. With hope in my heart I loved and cared for him as best as I could. The only holiday I took was a three day break that had already been booked previously. I only went because the lovely vet we had got to know throughout his treatment took him home with her! It was quite funny getting daily texts letting me know he was well!

Snowy then became diabetic and needed insulin. However, nine months after his original diagnosis, he was doing well enough that our regular vet felt we could cut down the visits. This was the news I wanted to hear! We shared a couple of months more before his condition gradually declined. I noticed he seemed to be getting quieter than usual but the hope did not leave me until one day I felt he needed to be seen, just to be sure. Our lovely vet was on holiday and the lady we saw did not know him well and could not tell me what was wrong. She took bloods and I insisted on the medication he had been given in the past hoping this would tide him over until our vet returned! He got progressively worse as the next few days went on, more calls, more visits, more medication, no change.

A week later he was clearly very ill and weak. I knew our vet was due back on the Monday - I was counting the hours till I could take him to her. I will never forget the feeling of both despair and hope I felt that day, as the words 'he has not got long' was devastating. So, here I was making a huge decision... leave him at the hospital for intensive treatment that might not save him, take him home with medication to ease his symptoms or euthanasia! All I remember thinking is I can't leave him, he will not spend his last days in a cage, alone! I took him home and hoped and hoped.

Two days later, although I don't remember agreeing, the inevitable was decided, and the vet was booked to come to our house. The medication had not made any difference; he was weak and not moving well. On his last night, I slept in the same room with him, nursing his every need. Even though he was terribly weak, my ever-round-boy still took the food and drink and cuddles I offered him!

The next morning I tried to put the vet off but she was firm and told me that a natural passing would be haunting to watch as he was in heart failure and it could be a long-drawn-out demise. We had three hours together before her visit. He was peaceful, serene and on his favourite blanket next to me as I gave him small amounts of all his favourite snacks and treats. I took him in my arms to our favourite seat in the garden and told him how much I loved him. The next hour was the most emotionally painful experience. Because of his heart failure, the injection was not working like it should and it all seemed prolonged and not such a peaceful end as I had imagined. The thought that this was his last moments here with me tore me apart and I was filled with guilt. I truly thought he would pass naturally and desperately didn't want him euthanised. I kept stroking him as if waiting for him to awake! The next few hours were in slow motion, we put him to rest in his garden with his favourite toy.

I cannot describe the depth of grief that followed. It was all consuming and overwhelming, physically painful and had a profound effect on my life. I was lost, looking for him constantly and felt so guilty. I kept playing the last days of his life over and over. The 'ifs and buts' were all I could think of! I was a wreck! A couple of months later more sadness, a very dear young member of the family passed tragically. This was the one person who had cried with me when I lost my boy, and now this lovely soul, who I loved dearly, was also gone. I was gripped by loss, grief and confusion! The finality of it all seemed so hard to accept!

What followed challenged my beliefs and emotions so greatly... Whilst engrossed in work sitting in my study, I suddenly looked up and for a fleeting moment and I saw a dark shadow move across from the door towards me into the room – the same size and shape as my dear boy! I instinctively knew it was him! It was just like how he would run in to find me and cosy up in the study! I could not believe it, I felt stunned, sceptical of my own mind but happy at the same time! Then one day I was browsing through a charity bookshop and came across a book on grief by a very special lady (who I was aware of) that works with children. Then, incredibly next to it, there was a book on pets and the afterlife!! I was taken aback, I had not been aware of this at all. I am by profession clinically trained, a career based on fact, evidence and logic! These books challenged my thoughts!

Then oddly, from not being aware of any psychic information and, to be honest, a sceptic, I happened to catch a TV show on the topic that caught my attention! Was it all a coincidence? I was grieving and in pain and I knew my husband sensed this but I tried to keep it contained! Then one day he told me he had taped a programme I would find interesting - it was about animal communication and the guest was the lovely Jackie! This touching and kind gesture by my husband led me to get in touch with Jackie.

The day of my appointment come, I was nervous, could this really work? I needn't have been. Jackie called and, as soon as I heard her voice, I felt relaxed. Her warmth came across. I felt like I was chatting to a friend! It felt natural and not shrouded in mystery or spooky in any way. She described my boy and his traits so accurately, even his swagger like a cartoon character. She initially suggested she felt his passing was uneventful, but I said I felt it was not but, as Jackie explained, although he was poorly, he was old and albeit the procedure had been slower than usual, he had not been in pain. My heart felt some ease at last. This is what I needed to know and she even named his illnesses but assured me again he had not experienced any pain.

She really relayed his essence and his message was of reminders of the fun times, our daily routines, the joy we shared, even where he sat in the garden! One message she gave me, no one could of known, it truly made me smile! Snowy then told Jackie he has a halo and was very proud of it! He was showing it to Jackie, we both enjoyed this and it made us laugh! I always knew he was an angel!! He made us both smile and the upbeat message was incredible. Jackie and I were now having a joyful chat reminiscing and not focusing on the passing!

Snowy mentioned about Christmas coming up and Jackie asked if I was looking for a decoration for the tree that seemed to be blue? I couldn't place this at time but it dawned on me afterwards that, a few months earlier I had bought a small Christmas angel, complete with a blue halo, and had put this on his resting place! I have to say, I then went out to find an angel for that years Christmas tree. The one I felt guided to was a glass tree-hanging ball containing a beautiful angel complete with a blue halo too! And the biggest connection is that of course Christmas is so significant as he was the best present ever.

Jackie told me he was well and looked young and healthy and was with another one of our past cats and even said the cat's name! Snowy even told me that he knew I was looking to get myself together and was thinking of booking a hair appointment and that he would be there with me! My tears turned to laughter! Lastly he showed Jackie a torn red heart turning pink! My dear Angel; he wanted me to know that my heart would heal and with that, he strolled off complete with his shining halo!

I was so uplifted and grateful for this experience, I also took great solace when I read a book written by Jackie with a very apt poem for those of us who lost our dear pets in similar ways. I later had the absolute pleasure of meeting Jackie in person. She is just as warm, friendly and a truly special person as I had thought during our call. Whilst I still miss my boy as much as ever and at times it is still overwhelmingly difficult, I feel Jackie, this incredibly empathetic, talented, lovely lady has touched my life greatly! Thank you Jackie

Letting Go

Your heart is bursting, searing with pain

That physical touch never to be had again

You only let them go because you so clearly care

They might not be here but they are surely up there.

You feel the pull and the tear of your heart
You feel torn inside and ripped apart
The enormity of choosing what best to do
It was done with your love, as they looked to you.

We don't enter into this without thought or care
We do it because the compassion is there
The choice to stop pain and distress of the one we love
Can only be guided by you and the angels above.

Many spirits have come through and given me their word
Your tears of sorrow and distress they heard
But they are free and happy and hold no ill will
Whatever was wrong could not have been cured with a pill.

The height of pain is a measuring device
It shows how deeply you felt throughout their life
With your love given for this most selfless act
They at least left this earth with their heart intact.

Now up yonder and free to roam
This is another level, like a new home
The day will come when you go up there too
They're ready and waiting to meet and embrace you.

If you truly did this from your genuine heart
You were so brave and helped them depart
Your love and courage was seen from above
This really was your strongest act of love.

If you could ask them now, what might they say?
"In my life, that was actually only one single day,
Please remember the rest, the joy, love and play,
For I look down from above and remember it that way."

As time has passed you may at last feel some ease
Maybe a pet has come for you to please
Animals are not selfish and want you to share
They left that space for another needing your love and care.

We are truly honoured to share in their space
Think back and let that smile adorn your face
The precious time you had could never be measured
Your lasting memories are of those you truly treasured.

Jackie Weaver 2009

*****

A lovely example of 'If an animal is going to come to you, they will!'...

Laura and her dog Ted

There are truly no words big enough to describe how much I loved Ted. He was my world. The day I met Ted I had not gone out with the intention of getting a dog, in fact, I was on my way to the garden centre with my sister when we passed a rundown looking kennels with a hand painted sign outside saying 'dogs needing homes'. We decided to go and have a nose around. It wasn't the nicest of places, bit dirty, bit smelly... we looked along the line of kennels, the sorry looking little furry faces, then, in between a very noisy Rottweiler and a very lively bull terrier sat a tiny little skinny grey boy, with hardly any fur, he was shaking like a leaf. The kennel worker opened the gate and he tentatively walked to the edge of the gate so we could stroke him. Then we left. I'd say I probably drove about five minutes down the road before I turned the car around and went back and got him. The kennel worker told us he had been picked up by the dog warden as a stray and they had shaved him as his fur was so matted; he'd had no vet checks or jabs since being with them. He had been picked up with another little dog, a Lhasa Apso, but this dog had been rehomed a couple of days beforehand.

On the way home we stopped at the pet shop and picked up everything we needed. The first thing we did when we got home was bath him; the poor little boy absolutely stank of urine. The cats were horrified to find I'd bought a dog home, and it took time and perseverance before everyone got along. When Ted went along for his first check-up, the vet put his age at around four years old and despite his start in life, and a slight skin condition, he was fine. Looking at him, we decided he was probably a Llasa Apso cross, as he was very similar to one.

Ted was my baby, he ruled the house, he slept in the bed, sat on the furniture, came pretty much everywhere with me. As time went by, Ted began to struggle with the back door step, I took him to the vets, they diagnosed arthritis in his back legs and lower back and he went on to have daily anti-inflammatories. It was during a back x-ray that they discovered he also had bladder stones, so he had an operation to remove them and more daily medication followed. Ted never complained about his ailments, he just got on with it. We were so close, and with so much change over the last few years: my fiancé leaving, my son moving away to university, losing my job, having to sell my home, I was so grateful to have him with me. It was just me and Ted. After a routine check-up at the vets, it was thought that the bladder stones had returned, so Ted was booked in for another operation, and it was during the pre-op scan that a growth was found in the adrenal gland, along with a few other things. The operation didn't go ahead and samples were sent off to a specialist. Ted was then diagnosed with Cushing's Disease. He was already on higher dose pain medication for his arthritis and now had cataracts forming in his eyes; I made the decision of no more operations and not to treat the Cushing's. My boy had been through enough, I wanted his time to be comfortable and stress free. One morning he wouldn't eat his breakfast and take his pain medication and his head felt very hot on one side so I took him the vet. Several tests revealed a vast amount of pressure behind the eyes and I was told he was in a lot of pain. I made the hardest decision of my life and my beautiful boy was put to sleep on 8th May 2014, he was eleven years old. I honestly thought I would die alongside him as my heart was ripped out. As I held him close I told him it was ok to go now and that I'd be fine, I wished him a safe journey, told him how much I loved him and how glad I was that we had found each other and thanked him for letting me be his Mum.

During the last few months of Ted's illness I had read various books on animal communication in an attempt to see if I could master it myself. I wanted to be sure Ted wasn't in pain and that he was happy to still be here - I hated the thought of him hanging on in pain for my sake. However, I never managed to do it and put it down to being too emotionally involved to be able to connect. When Ted passed away I was so distraught I did a search on the internet for spirit animal readings and came across Jackie, I didn't hesitate, I paid my money and sent her an email. The reading was booked for a couple of weeks later. I didn't think I could wait that long, but looking back, I'm glad it wasn't right away as I was a lot calmer by the time the day came. I was nervous and excited on the day of the reading; I kept telling Ted that we were going to have a chat real soon (I still talk to him as if he's here).

Jackie started by saying what a gentle soul Ted was, and he truly was, he didn't have a bad bone in his body. Then she said; 'He's showing me a pram, why would a dog show me a pram?' This made me laugh as the weekend before Ted passed away I really wanted to go to the local garden show, I didn't want to leave Ted at home on his own. I knew his legs wouldn't cope with that amount of walking, so I took him in a doggy stroller... and one of the wheels fell off! Ted had a lovely time sitting in the pram whilst I spend the day trying to push him around a field on three wheels; it was a memorable funny day.

Jackie then went on to tell me that Ted never felt like he was a burden, and everything I did, I did because I loved him. He even said that I didn't really go out often and sometimes there were things I might have wanted to do, but I didn't, but knew I was okay with that. This was so true, I rarely went out because I wouldn't leave him; if friends asked me along to things my mantra was pretty much 'Sorry, I can't leave Ted'. Also, I did everything for him: if he got tired I carried him, if he didn't fancy his dinner I'd cook him something else, if he was having a bad night, I'd sit up with him until he settled again. This was one of the things I needed confirmation of, that Ted knew how much I loved him.

She also talked about his food, blankets, toys, all were spot on. She said she felt she had a tick list of ailments and it was like ticking off each illness as it came along. She said she felt his front legs were aching, not in pain, just achy. Teds arthritis was in his back end, which made it hard for his back legs to get going; he would do a quick step with his front legs to get the back ones in stride, his front legs would do all the work and he would get tired quickly, which is why we only had short walks each day, another thing Jackie picked up on.

Jackie asked if I was a carer, I'm not, but I was up until about three months ago! She said my present job has a lot of paper, that it's not as computerised as it could be. This made me laugh, you wouldn't believe the paperwork! I'm a PA and even the diary is a paper book taped to the desk! It's like I've gone back in time. She said I need fulfilment, that my current job doesn't give me that (and she's right), she said I need to go back to some sort of caring, either as a job or as a volunteer, as that's where my fulfilment is. She then said 'Ted says you shouldn't work in customer service, it's not you.' Again, this made me laugh - me and customer service are really not a good match.

Jackie said Ted was showing her a Lhasa Apso and asked if I'd had another dog which she felt had passed to spirit. Ted was saying they were together again and I told Jackie that Ted had been picked up by the dog warden with a little mate of that breed but they had been rehomed separately. It's good to know they have been reunited.

Jackie said Ted was telling her there was no body, which of course relates to him being cremated, but she said she felt like there was a rose on his casket, maybe a rose for love? I didn't understand this as I hadn't placed a rose on his casket. It wasn't until a couple of days ago that it clicked with me. I don't have a rose on his casket, but I do have a rose quartz crystal next to it, which I placed there for peace and love.

"What is this 'popping to the shops' Ted is saying?" Jackie asked me, 'did you pop to the shops?' … If I had to go out, I always told Ted where I was going, how long I would be, what time I was aiming to be home... then she said 'but why is he saying it like that, it's not like your voice?' Jackie did a little mimic of how Ted was saying it, this made me laugh as I did have a 'Ted voice' when I spoke to him and I if I was going shopping I always said to him 'Mums just popping to the shops Teddy, won't be long'.

Jackie said that Ted was saying we'd both had to brave the day he passed, that he knew it was time and that my broken heart will heal. He said I'm about to start the next chapter of my life, and there will be lots of change. He said we were two halves that made a whole, that he had had a full life experience with me and that I had given him eternal peace. What more could I ask for, my boy was now at peace.

Jackie said 'You might think this sounds a bit odd, but he's asking if you've seen the lights in the corner of the bedroom?'... and I had! The night before the reading there were tiny quick sparks of white light up by the ceiling. "That's him," said Jackie "That's him flitting around you."

Jackie was spot on with everything she told me. I can't begin to tell you how amazing and comforting it was to speak to my Ted, he was my baby, my life and I am so grateful to Jackie for sharing her gift. After the reading I looked at the photograph I have of Ted next to the TV and smiled... and that tiny flash of white light flickered back at me from just above the photo frame.

*****

An Angel of a cat that changed their lives forever...

Tara and Peter's cat Lilly

It was a sunny afternoon in June, and we were out in the garden sitting by the barbeque having a glass of wine. We heard a meow, and a pretty little black and white cat appeared, trotting along the top of the fence. She was very friendly and we all shared some chicken together. We noticed she had a little black smudge under her nose that made her look like she had a little moustache and an identical black patch on each little white front leg which exactly matched when she stood with her legs together. As we sat, we wondered, was she a neighbour's cat? I had a feeling though and jokingly said to my wife, "That's your cat that is".

And so it turned out to be, though at that time we really didn't know, where she had come from. As evening came on we went inside and left her by the barbeque. She stayed for hours looking at the place where we had sat, and it seemed like she had enjoyed her afternoon and didn't want to go. Over the next few weeks, she would turn up again and sat outside our door looking in. We became concerned in case she really had no home so we let her in a couple of times and fed her.

Then one night she came to sit on our doorstep under the porch. We put fleeces out for her to sleep on, still unsure as to whether she belonged to anyone. Looking back we feel bad about it, but we really didn't know at the time. That night it rained but we didn't think she would still be sitting there through it all - we were wrong. In the morning, there she was sitting on damp fleeces and a bit wet but generally bright and cheerful and pleased to see us. That was it. We brought her in, fed her and made a fuss of her. We gave her a name, Lilly, and we loved her.

At first she lived outside in the day while we were at work. We had made a place for her in the shed and we took her to the vet to see if she had a microchip. We didn't even have a carrier to take her in, so we just popped her in the car in an open box. We prayed that she was nobody's because by then we were so fond of her and wanted her to stay.

We remember how relieved we were when we found that she wasn't microchipped, but the vet took her details in case anyone was looking for her. Much to our relief, it soon became apparent she was a stray. We remember that night, her sitting on the shelf in the back of the car, looking out at us while we went into to a large pet superstore to get her some things.

We had never had a cat before, or any pet since childhoods, and it was a learning curve for us all. She had chosen us and it was a special relationship from the start. She wasn't going to live outside all day it seemed, she made that plain, so we made a bed for her in the kitchen. That lasted one day! So she had the run of the house after that, and slept where she liked. This turned out to be our bed, not just on it, but in it with us! We resisted, but it was useless. You should have seen the smug look on her face when she finally made it. From stray cat to pampered pet, not bad eh!

Lilly was such a smart little cat and thought to be around twelve years old. Over the months we came to know each other well - she would talk constantly and would always answer when you spoke to her, or asked her anything. Such as…

Q: Lilly, how do you want your beef, Rare? (No answer) Well done? (No answer) Medium rare? This option would be answered with a meow. She even learned to put up her paw when she wanted a treat. She had a fascination with water and liked to drink from a glass so, at night time, she drank from her own personal glass that we had given her! She would sit and wait for us at bedtime, and watch impatiently if we were late. In the early hours she liked to roam about the house. On the bedside table is our clock, it has a sensor which switches on a blue light behind the face when you wave your hand over it. Lilly frequently set this off by climbing on the bedside cabinet and sitting over it, after a while I think she got the hang of it just fine.

We even taught her to wear a little harness with the intention of taking her for walks. Other people didn't believe we could teach her to wear it. Not an older cat surely they thought, but she did wear it. It took a couple of months, with patience and encouragement and in the end she would stand patiently while her "little jacket" as we called it was fitted. She seemed to wear it proudly.

There were a few visits to the vet. On one occasion she seemed to react badly to an injection, but she recovered and we all enjoyed our Christmas together at the end of 2012. The New Year started well, but then Lilly appeared to be drinking more than usual and seemed to struggle jumping up on to the bed. Fortunately we were just moving into our re-decorated bedroom and the bed wasn't in there at first so we had the mattress on the floor which, being low, made it easier for Lilly. Sadly she got worse: she stopped eating, seemed distant, was drinking more, but losing weight all the time. We took her to the vet, not imagining we would never see her again. The vet kept her in for tests. They called us that afternoon, a Saturday. The tests had shown that Lilly had severe kidney disease and would have to be put to sleep. At the time they called us she was still drowsy from the anaesthetic they had given her. We felt it was kinder to let her go then in her drowsy state, than prolong her suffering by going back to the vets to see her. The worst part was we never really said goodbye to her, just, "See you later Lilly". But we never saw her again and we were heartbroken at her going.

We never realised how a little animal could affect a person's life. Many people have experienced this, but the awful sense of loss was a new experience for us. It was humbling; we have never looked at animals the same way since.

It was some time before we decided to contact Jackie. We read about her gift on the internet, and what others had said about her. I was open minded, but my wife was convinced that Jackie could talk with Lilly, and I wanted to help her if I could.

Jackie contacted us in the evening through Skype, it was nice to be able to see her and both of us talk. She had already contacted Lilly and straight away she began to relay what Lilly was saying to her. It was truly fascinating to hear from her point of view. She was truly grateful to us for giving her a home. That she had been attracted by the fact that we didn't have dogs! She had hung around but 'wasn't pushy'. We laughed at this, but it was true, Lilly had waited politely at the door until we invited her in.

Jackie asked Lilly about the time before she came to us. She said she had been with an old lady she loved and had been called a name like Fluffy. She described a removal van, an empty house, and becoming homeless. Jackie asked us if during the weeks before she moved in with us, she had disappeared for a while. We remembered we had not seen her for well over a week during that time and thought she had gone home. In fact this was true, she told Jackie she had gone back, but the house was empty and there was no one there, so she came back to us.

She described herself as our 'little ray of sunshine', and how she had 'taught us loads.' How ironic, there was us thinking how it was us who had taught her!

What struck me was how Lilly's perspective on things was different to ours, a simpler and very honest rational.

We talked about her little jacket, and asked if she liked it. Lilly was showing Jackie something that she said 'hugged her', and she knew that we wanted her to wear it to keep her safe when she went out. She described it as her 'life jacket' and simply said "It worked!" How aptly put, I thought. "Going for a walk like a dog", she said "But I'm not a dog". Lilly didn't like dogs!

If you ever talk to Jackie you will know that she means what she is telling you, and she will just let you know what she is being told as she hears it. Pieces sometimes come through detached but then things will begin to join up and this is when magical moments will occur. Such a moment was when we talked about Lilly drinking from a glass. Jackie thought it was funny as she was seeing a special glass and asked if it was actually crystal. No, it wasn't but it was a faceted glass, catching the light. Lilly had described her glass. With the wonders of being on webcam, I was able to show Jackie Lilly's glass, and it was just as she had said.

The thing that worried us was the fact that we never said goodbye to her and we wondered if Lilly had thought we had abandoned her. She said to Jackie that she knew she had a tumour on her kidney, it had come on quickly, and that she had heard us say to the vet to do whatever tests were necessary to find the problem. She had also said to Jackie that we had picked up on her illness really quickly when others would not have, and that she knew we had not abandoned her. The vet had told us the same thing that we had picked up on the illness very quickly, because cats hide their pain very well. However, we had never told Jackie about what the vet had said, or about the tests and the anaesthetic, but she knew through Lilly what had happened there. Jackie repeated Lilly's words, "I just drifted away." Would she ever visit us again, was a question we asked. We had only known her for nine months. Jackie asked her for us. Lilly replied, "I have lots to do here and lots of visits to make." This was meant for people and animals, and apparently she has met Jackie's Stan too!

Then Jackie said she was seeing a light flashing on and off, she didn't know what it was, perhaps a computer screen, but a light of some sort. Then she held her hand out and started moving it from side to side. "I'm seeing this sort of action" she said "and some sort of light." It was another of those great moments when the pieces come together. It was the bedside clock, being the type you wave your hand over to get it to come on, or go off. A couple of days after Lilly died, the light had come on a couple of times in the night. A faulty sensor? Perhaps, but we felt not as you have to get your hand really close to that clock to get the light to work. But more to the point, we had never ever mentioned the clock and the light to Jackie, but here was Lilly telling Jackie that it was her that was switching the blue light on, as she had done before. Yes she had visited, and still does now and then.

The experience was an uplifting one for us, and it completed a story that started in June 2012 and opened a new door for us. It made us realise that a bond with an animal doesn't just end when they die. We don't forget them and they obviously don't forget us either. We still get sad from time to time but also have a laugh at the funny things that have happened.

We emailed Jackie a couple of days after the talk. We wanted Lilly to know that we felt honoured to have had her. Stan had said, "She is a shining star here too, just send the thought, she will hear you."

We are now volunteers at the local cat rescue centre and have now got another little black and white cat called Sylvie; she has her own very individual personality and she will benefit from Lilly, as thanks to her, we are in no doubt that animals do understand what you say.

On the weekend Sylvie arrived, the blue light came on again several times and we just knew who was doing that. We may only have had her nine months, but what she brought to our life has enriched us beyond words.

*****

'Forever is forever'

Lynne and her Dog Jorja

I have had Golden Retrievers (less formally known as 'goldies') for years, I just fell in love with the breed.

After my goldie Chloe passed away followed weeks later by my Dad, life felt very sad. I still had my dog Layla but felt the tug for a new puppy. I got in touch with Wendy, who was a well respected breeder and she put me on her waiting list. Several months later I had a phone call -a litter of eleven pups had been born, but with only two girls and another lady had first choice! After lots of visits the great day arrived to collect my puppy, who I had decided to call Jorja (Jorjie). As Wendy opened the outside pen, eleven bundles of joy came spilling out. I picked up the one closest to me, turned the puppy over and said jokingly "Oh it's a girl, it must be mine." Wendy said, "Yes that one is yours, the other lady has already chosen her one." I fell in love on the spot.

I brought her home and she was an exceptional puppy, no crying at night, not one toilet accident in the house, and no chewing (I never had one before of since that didn't chew!). She grew into a beautiful adult dog, with impeccable manners. She was all about love and kindness and that even included chasing rabbits she could easily have caught, but never did.

When she was eight years old, she had to have a lump removed from her shoulder and, devastatingly, the vet said the prognosis wasn't good. Jorjie wasn't having any of that... My darling girl lived another six years, to just a few short weeks of her fifteenth birthday. It broke my heart to say goodbye to her, but I knew it was time. I always think of her as my heart dog. I have loved and adored each and every dog I have had, but she had that extra special something.

I have been interested in animal communication for a many years and Jackie and I had been Facebook friends for a number of years too. It turned out we had a connection through horse racing too - my Dad used to own racehorses who were trained by Toby Balding OBE who is featured in her *Celebrity Pet Talking* book.

For the anniversary of Jorjas passing, I decided to have a reading with Jackie.

91

A few days later Jackie rang... She described Jorja to a tee and said Jorja was telling her that I had been looking at lots of scarves. This was so true! The previous day I had been at a street market in Bath, doing just that!

Jackie said that she was being shown a sort of statue, which she thought was in our garden. I knew instantly what she was describing; we have a puppy sized stone goldie in the garden I bought around the time I got her. Jorja said she would like her name on a plaque near it, and I will be delighted to do that in her honour. Jackie could also picture her running round and round and round! She did a lot of running about like that which often was in a figure-of-eight. (I call it 'the scats' which is a sign of a happy dog.) Jackie also said Jorja wasn't a dog for running off and would get itchy skin. Both right; she did suffer with wet eczema.

Jackie then said she was showing her a sandy bank that seemed very significant. Wow! I used to take her to a beach in Dorset called... SANDBANKS! She simply adored that beach and I took her there not long before her last day on Earth. She volunteered that she passed on a sunny day, which she did. I can remember through my tears the golden rays still shone bright.

It was such a lovely heartfelt reading and I know Jackie truly got the essence of my girl. Jorja also told Jackie to tell me 'Forever is Forever' meaning love never dies. So yes, in essence, Forever is Forever' as our love *is* forever. Such beautiful and meaningful words which are perfect for her plaque by the statue too.

A few days later as I was driving to the local shops with the radio on (I only listen to the radio in the car) and was thinking about my reading when, all of a sudden, the song *Time in a Bottle* by Jim Croce came on. Another wow moment and you might wonder why this would be. But, back when I lost her, I heard it then and felt the words of that song just captured all I felt about her. So, I wrote out all the lyrics on a card and then left it where I scattered her ashes.

The story doesn't quite end there, because when I returned home and switched my laptop on, I noticed the date... it was Jorjas birthday! You couldn't make it up could you?! I feel even closer than ever to Jorja, which I could never have thought possible, so thank you Jackie and thank you precious girl for choosing me to spend your time on earth with. You came at exactly the right time and helped ease the grief and sadness that was rocking our lives back then. God bless until we meet again... Forever is forever!!

*****

A chance to say 'Goodbye'...

Yvonne and her dog Mindy

When I first met Mindy I was in the breeder's home watching two little girl pups playing with each other. I was wondering which one I would feel more drawn too. The breeder and I were chatting away, when suddenly she said to me, "I think it's *you* who has been picked!" There, snuggled up in my lap, was Mindy and from that moment on my heart was hers.

I got Mindy at twelve weeks old and she was a tiny red sable, long-haired, Chihuahua. She may have been a little girl but what she lacked in size, she sure made up with personality! From the start she was so loyal, a constant companion, always busy and facing life full on and ready to take part in what ever we offered her.

Mindy was so loving and liked nothing better than to cuddle up on someone's lap but, as is often said about Chihuahuas, she was a big dog in a small dog's body and was not afraid to challenge any dog that crossed her path! One day, much to my dismay, she demonstrated this whilst walking across the fields - suddenly a Rottweiler appeared behind her, and she wanted to let it know who was boss! Thankfully, the Rottweiler just looked at her with utter disgust and moved on and I breathed a huge sigh of relief.

All the family loved her and over the years she gave us many laughs and many stories to put in our memory box. For almost ten years she was in good health but the last year she had definitely slowed down. She became a late riser in the mornings, and after calling to her several times, she would reluctantly appear, do what she had to do, have her breakfast and then quite happily retire back to bed. At times she was still very playful and would race around playing with the other dogs but she did seem to tire quicker and pant more. Was it just old age creeping up on her? I started to feel concerned so decided to take her to the vets and have her checked out. They examined her, asked various questions and said nothing seemed to be wrong - a sense of relief washed over me and life continued as normal.

Then one morning, I awoke to find Mindy having problems breathing, so I called the vets immediately and arranged to meet them at an out-of-hours surgery. With tears in my eyes and sheer panic in my heart, I drove as best as I could. We were literally only two minutes from the surgery when my beloved girl passed over in my husband's arms. I was absolutely devastated.

Over the next couple of weeks, I was grieving for Mindy but with that was a mix of guilt as I kept wondering, 'Did I miss something? Were there signs of an illness?' I couldn't shake off this nagging feeling and it was taking over my grieving. I said to my husband 'I wish I could talk to a clairvoyant and through her, talk to Mindy.' I decided to look on the internet for a clairvoyant (not knowing anything about animal communicators) and thankfully my search and research led me to Jackie Weaver.

On the morning of my reading with Jackie I was very nervous and anxious. I was desperate for it to go well and wondered if Mindy would even communicate? Well, I shouldn't have worried as true to form, Mindy had plenty to say. Jackie was so calm and easy to talk to. I relaxed immediately. When Jackie told me that Mindy said she had a 'big personality' and felt like she would have been top dog, I knew she was talking to my little girl. Although we had five dogs, we always said she was top dog.

It was such a relief for me to hear from Jackie, that Mindy said that I must let go of the guilt as there were no signs of an illness and that she was well until the end. Mindy also said that she was glad that no illness had been found when she was checked as she loved living her life in the way she did and wouldn't have wanted her lifestyle to change. She said that although I was finding it hard that she went so quickly; it was better that way than a long drawn out illness and, in time, when I was feeling stronger, I would see this as a blessing too.

I laughed when Jackie told me that Mindy said she was 'a good example and that the other dogs should follow' and that she was 'very intelligent.' I could just imagine her blowing her own trumpet. (They are not all small dogs - one is much larger - she is our adorable spaniel. Mindy told Jackie that she was not a 'loop the loop' type, and so true, she is a very sensible spaniel and loved by all the dogs.) I laughed also when Mindy said the words to Jackie 'MY bedroom.' She had her own little bed in our room - this was her safe haven and she quickly decided it was her room where I was a welcome guest but not so my husband! Every night they would go through the same ritual - she would wait at the top of the stairs for him, then moan and grumble at him, before comfortably retiring off to bed herself.

Jackie painted for me a beautiful picture of Mindy with her sister in spirit world, I was so happy to hear that they were together again. When I'm feeling sad and missing her, I love to conjure up an image of her and Tilly running through the meadow together. It was so lovely to hear that she knew I had a special spark for her and that she thought that I gave extra special treatment.

My three way conversation with Jackie and Mindy made me cry, made me laugh, and gave me the answers I needed. Most importantly for me, because Mindy had been taken so quickly, Jackie brought Mindy to life for me and gave me a chance to say goodbye - I hadn't been able to do it properly at the time and this had been breaking my heart. This communication has given me such peace. Thank you so much Jackie.

*****

Huge dog, huge heart, huge love…

Kim and her Dog Lenny

Having owned German Shepherds all my life it was the breed I was used to, so, when my last shepherd passed away, all I thought about was getting another one. But, as fate had it, I was watching the Paul O'Grady TV show one evening and he was doing an item about dogs. I saw this marvellous huge chunk of a dog and didn't even know what breed it was, but what I did know was, that was going to be my next type of dog!

Having trawled the web to find out what breed it was I came across a site about Newfoundlands. I had found them! These were the same breed I'd seen on his show. I was smitten. People advised me against getting such a huge dog but I was determined to get one even though I knew nothing about their breed but was willing to take on board anything extra I needed to know. With more searching I found an advert of some of these puppies for sale. I contacted the breeder and I, and my daughter, went along that Saturday to see them.

Whoosh! In came this huge dog with a personality to match – she was the mother of the puppies and truly gorgeous. Her size didn't put me off; she was big and bouncy but sensible with it. I will never forget the moment I went in to see the puppies… There was my boy! He was the biggest one in the litter, was laid down just looking at me with his huge brown eyes. My heart just melted. People do say you should go with the puppy that comes running to you so I asked if I could hold him. Wow, when I did, was he so heavy and only was eight weeks old! I fell in love with him there and then.

When I got him home he was so laid back. He seemed to lie down a lot and he would only play for 15 minutes and then have to have a nap. This struck me as unusual for a puppy but as I got to know Lenny, I found out that was just his laid back nature. My daughter and myself loved having Lenny; he was so gorgeous and quickly grew into a big beautiful boy. He was a gentle soul that took life at his pace. He was a giant of a dog with a giant personality to match. Lenny always did something to make us laugh with his happy sunny personality. He was a very joyful dog with the most expressive eyes and I have never known a dog that could talk so much! I thought he must have been part human. Lenny loved playing with his cuddly toys and he adored children and would always lie down so they could cuddle him.

When Lenny was three-years-old, I decided to buy him a puppy friend and, needless to say, I bought another Newfoundland. We named him Ronnie. When we bought him home, Lenny sniffed his new friend and was obviously unsure of him. We quickly went and bought a playpen so we could put Ronnie in it so Lenny could get used to him that way. This didn't quite go to plan - we laughed and laughed when we saw that Lenny had gone and sat in there himself to escape from the new pup! Soon enough, Lenny realised that Ronnie was not replacing him but was a friend for him. They became best friends and totally inseparable. They happily played together and enjoyed walks and going to the country shows.

As the years went by, Lenny was then eight years old and I began to notice he was starting to walk like a mechanical toy with his front legs. I first I thought it was his arthritis (which sadly he did have) but as the months went on I soon became to realise that it was more serious than that. So, off we went to the vets, where he had every test they could do. To my surprise all the tests came back negative and they could not find what was wrong with him. The vets concluded that he had Myasthenia Gravis (an auto-immune neuromuscular disease) but we later found out this was not the case. It turned out that he had a dog version of Motor Neurone Disease.

We were determined to do everything to help him get better, or at least try and halt it in its tracks. Sadly, as the months went on, it became apparent that the disease was affecting his back legs too. He could now no longer walk properly on any legs. Although we were heartbroken we were still determined not to give up. Having taken a lot of advice, we invested in a special harness so we could support/carry him to and from the garden and anywhere else he needed. We started taking him to hydrotherapy lessons as we still hoped that he would beat this disease.

One morning I came down the stairs and found that Lenny could not move. I immediately phoned the vets to ask them to come out to see him. When the vets arrived they told me the news I dreaded hearing. They said there was nothing more they could do for him and that's when I knew that I had to let him go. So, with my heart in a thousand pieces, I agreed and he went to sleep, forever.

Overwhelmed with grief at this time I didn't know who to turn too or what to do. All I could think about was that I needed to speak to him; I so desperately wanted to ask him loads of questions and also deal with the questions I needed answering in my own head too. So, back on the internet once again but this time I was not looking for puppies, I was looking for an animal psychic and that is where I noticed one women that stood out for me - her name being Jackie Weaver. I went on her website, read lots of things other people had said of her work and instantly emailed her. I am so glad I did. We arranged a phone call although I didn't know what to expect from this reading, but it had been two weeks since he passed over so I so dearly hoped he would come through.

Jackie connected to Lenny straight away. She didn't need to ask me anything because Lenny did most of the talking just like he did when he was here with us! It was so emotional for me to hear the things he was talking to me about like when he won a rosette at a country show and that he loved everyday he spent with his family. He talked about his physical problems and thanked us for all that we did for him. He said he was never miserable and he knew how much we tried but in the end, the disease got the better of him and he simply gave up the fight. I was relieved having it confirmed that we really had no choice left for him.

He also mentioned that my daughter and I had been looking at pictures and watching videos of him which was so true - we had been looking at them for a few days leading up to the call. Jackie remarked that she was quite surprised by this saying many people cannot bear to even look at photos, let alone videos, but how lovely that he had been watching them, watching him. He made me laugh because he wanted to point out that he was more intelligent than my other Newfoundland, Ronnie, and he was! Ronnie is lovely but Lenny was clearly the smarter boy.

He also talked about how my daughter loved cuddle him (she was always doing that) and that I called him 'mummy's big bear' which was spot on. Jackie also told me that Lenny was in the kindergarten in Heaven looking after children who had passed. Well, that was Lenny all over; he loved kids and always wanted to be cuddled by them. There was so much said and it was just wonderful to hear it relayed to me.

Jackie asked if his breed was the same type as the rescue dogs you see in pictures with the brandy barrels under their neck. I said yes and they were in fact, water rescue dogs. Jackie paused and said he wasn't making her feel terribly keen on water - that was so true as he only ever liked a paddle but would never actually swim! We laughed saying it was just as well he hadn't been called upon to help rescue a drowning person.

Jackie is a really lovely lady; she put me at ease with the communication and what she was saying no one else could have known about the relationship between Lenny and me. I really did find it a great comfort to be able to talk to him and to know that he is still with us and is watching over us.

It was a remarkable reading and I can't thank Jackie enough. I will be forever truly grateful to her.

*****

And another animal that came, wanted or not...

Penny and her Cat Toffee

I met Toffee, when she was just a few days old. My daughter's cat had three kittens, Toffee being the sweet tiny tortoiseshell one, just so adorable! She grew into the prettiest cat you would ever see.

I had a black and white cat called Cheekie, my loving and constant companion through many difficult times in my life, who died in 1999 aged nearly fourteen. I was devastated and could not cope and eventually sought help from a counsellor from an Animal Sanctuary.

At that time my daughter was expecting her second child, and was concerned that Toffee, who had got into the first child's cot when it was a baby, would do the same again. Looking back, I feel that it was an excuse for me to have Toffee because she knew of the grief I was experiencing and thought it would help with my sadness. (I am so grateful to her now although I wasn't really at the time.) She asked if I would have Toffee because of 'her worry' but I was reluctant; I felt it was too soon after Cheekie's death. I did not feel ready but she persisted and Toffee, who was just over four years old, came to live with me anyway.

She was so different from Cheekie - I was still grieving for him but we loved her and she soon settled in. She had only been with us for a few weeks, when one night (she was used to going in and out herself at night) I was woken by a strange sound. I went downstairs and she had been sick outside, came in and slept for the rest of the day. About 5pm she suddenly became very ill, vomiting and passing fluid - very frightening. We rushed her to our veterinary hospital where upon examination they were terribly concerned as it became apparent that she had suffered some sort of accident/trauma. She was in a very bad way and needed emergency surgery there and then. They explained there was a chance she would not get through it and that it would be very expensive. I couldn't have cared less how much it was, she had to be given the chance so we left her in their capable hands and spent a worrying evening waiting for the vet's phone call.

The vet phoned late that evening. She had a ruptured bladder along with other internal injuries but had come through the operation but not without an extremely close call... She had stopped breathing, and just as they were ready to call it a day, she started breathing again. The love I had felt for her deepened; I had nearly lost her and she had survived; we were meant to be together! She did so well and the vet was so pleased with her progress. She healed well and was soon back to her happy and inquisitive self.

She was a joy: my baby, my special friend, my clown, and my life. When she was diagnosed with cancer, the bottom fell out of my world. We brought her home after the diagnosis and she lived for a few weeks comfortably, until she died on December 9th 2011. She was put to sleep at the veterinary hospital, the circumstances I still do not want to think about - we wanted her put to sleep at home but, due to things outside our control, this could not happen.

We brought her home and she is buried under the garden seat where she loved to sit. The seat has a plaque in her memory, and her grave has pretty flowers growing there all year. She was nearly thirteen and my tears still flow. Her little basket of toys are still in the same place, photos are everywhere. She will be with me forever.

I was told about Jackie by a close friend and so I got in touch with her for some reassurance that Toffee was at peace and that the love we shared would never die.

I felt nervous waiting for Jackie's phone call, but soon felt comfortable with her loving voice and kindness. She found Toffee very easy to get in contact with and that was typical of Toffee; she was always ready to join in everything.

She talked of Toffee exactly as I knew her and her funny little ways and nosiness came through. She talked about a 'scratching' noise. This sound was made on the bottom stair carpet and she knew exactly what she was doing; she would scratch to get my attention, look at me, then run off up the stairs as if it was a game. I asked Jackie if she could ask her about the accident she had had and she told her she had fallen. I had suspected that all along; the vet had said she thought she had been hit by something, but we live in a small road off a main road, so there was hardly any traffic in the early hours of the morning. I believe now she had maybe lost her balance in one of the high trees and hurt herself landing or even crashed into branches on the way down. We will never truly know but thank goodness she came home and didn't run off in fright.

Toffee talked of pretty flowers. Jackie said she thought they were maybe Primroses, Primulas she was being shown. Yes, they were. Those were the flowers we put on her grave. As we closed out chat, Jackie said Toffee said, "She is still your baby." I had always called her that!

Jackie's chat opened up a new belief of the deep love and eternal closeness we have with our departed pets. Some strange little incidents have happened since she died, confirming her presence is always near, and our love for one another will never die.

Thank you Jackie for the comfort you have given me.

*****

An adorable boy off on his adventures..

Adrienne and her cat Frodo

I was distraught after losing my beautiful Frodo, only aged seven, through complications from Chronic Renal Failure. He was a dusky pink Maine Coon cross and everybody who met him loved him. I decided to contact Jackie because she was mentioned in a book I read about reincarnated animals and I just wanted my boy back so much. When Jackie called me, she had already connected to him.

She described him as the gentlest of souls. He would sit on the back of the sofa and would kiss you, if you put your face up to his. Jackie said that he always thought of himself as a kitten and had a big personality. Then Jackie said it couldn't be sure she was right, but was he more like a dog than a cat? When I reassured her that he really did act like a dog (playing fetch and growling at the postman), she laughed. Then the phone went silent for a moment as he spoke to Jackie and then she repeated his words, 'There will never be another one like me, but there was never supposed to be another one like me.' That brought tears to my eyes.

Jackie said that we still felt him in the house (true) and that he would be with me in the kitchen (where I have my favourite photo of him). She described him dashing for the litter tray - which is what he would do as a kitten. He'd play and then only realise at the last minute that he needed to go and had to rush like the clappers to the tray.

Frodo had Reiki healing though his illness and Jackie said that he used to feel the energy go up from his feet and through his body. Frodo told her that I could not have stopped him getting the disease and that all the injections and pills were just a process which he knew he had to go through. He said that he had to leave me because he was a healing cat and he could now do so much for other cats in need.

Frodo said that he had passed over peacefully and gave her the image of the sun (the sun was setting as he passed but he couldn't have known as he'd been in at the vets since the night before and the room where he passed had no windows). Jackie then asked if it was his kidneys that were the problem. I'd not said anything about this but confirmed it and I asked him to forgive me for making the decision to put him to sleep. He said there was nothing to forgive as it was just one tiny moment in a lifetime of happiness.

Frodo told Jackie that he was such a special part of my life and that could never be taken away. His next words were, 'I had a beautiful existence and don't grieve for me as I am still here.'

He then showed Jackie, children's windmills and was being all bouncy and smiley. Frodo was always happiest being a jungle cat out in the garden, and then I realised... in the last few weeks he seemed to prefer to wee by the large windmill my daughter planted in my veg patch! He must have thought it was hilarious!

Jackie said he was saying "30" and "birthday" - she asked me if there was something special about my 30th Birthday but after lots of thinking, I finally remembered my own birth date is the 30th!

I wanted to know if he was coming back to me, as in the book I had read, but he said, 'No, I can't. I'm too busy.' He said that he would be my guardian angel always but he wouldn't be coming back to Earth because he could do so much more from where he was. He talked about the other cats I have and said that they were fine without him.

To my young daughter, who didn't get a chance to say goodbye, he said 'be adventurous' and asked me to give her a kiss from him, which is just what she needed.

His last words to me were: 'I'm fine and I know you needed to hear that from me.' He was right, I most certainly did. Bless you Frodo and enjoy all the wonderful work you'll do in Heaven.

*****

May her loss not be in vain...

Kim and her dog Cassie

After losing our beloved dog, Tammy, in 2004, my Mum and I began the search for our Cassie. We searched for a number of weeks until finally we found her at Dogs Trust in Newbury, quite a way from home. The second I saw her; I knew she was ours. The moment we met, I knew that I already knew her. She stood up, put her paws very gently on my chest and we looked into each other's eyes – it was if she knew she was coming home. I felt we must have been together in Heaven and had finally found each other again. The day we collected her, she was brought out to us on a lead, tail wagging, smiling, and she stood up and put her paws very gently on my chest: she knew she was coming home. Tears of joy were falling on my cheeks.

We had Cassie with us on earth for five years. She was almost a year old when we got her. Being a collie, she was into everything and went everywhere she could with me. She was a very loving, gentle dog with the most beautiful eyes you ever saw. We understood each other easily. Wherever we went people were drawn to her. She could "talk" to people. She had her hyper collie moments when she would charge around the garden with a toy, or around the park playing and herding her dog friends; she could almost out run the greyhounds when she was younger (I think she had a little of that breed in her somewhere). At the weekends we'd do extra long walks along the river. She loved meeting the wildlife, and thanks to her we rescued a number of birds.

Cassie was also my protector. My hearing was damaged when I was younger, resulting in what is now, a severe loss. She had excellent hearing so, in her own way, she became my hearing dog. She would always tell me if something was going on and would protect me from strangers. We looked out for each other; we went through a lot together. I will always love my Cassie with all my heart and soul. She was my life, my world. Even though she is now in Heaven, that bond will never break.

Cassie went to Heaven one evening, Wednesday 2nd December 2009. We were on our usual walk along the fields by the river. Cassie went into bushes and never came back. Somehow she had got onto the railway lines and was killed by a train.

It didn't make any sense, none of it. Cassie had simply vanished. The railway line was supposedly fenced off behind the bushes and streams; it was a designated town park. We had walked here for years. She had only been out of view for a few seconds as an express train shot past and through the station. Logic was saying it couldn't have happened but I just knew something was wrong. I screamed her name and felt a stab in my heart. What made matters worse was; because of my hearing loss, I was unable to listen for any signs of her or hear anybody that could have helped me either.

There is no way I can describe the horror of that night and the loss overwhelmed me. I just wanted to go with her. I was so distraught and there was no one around to help me. Eventually, I got my friend, Annette, to help me search whilst Mum waited at home, just in case. We searched through the night and at first light I checked with the station and they said no dog has been reported. I was trying to tell people that she was dead but it was so unbelievable, no one believed me. I HAD to find her. I was in such a state of stress and panic I almost lost my ability to speak. So we put Cassie on a missing dog's website – DogLost.co.uk. We searched day and night along with Cassie's friends, both human and canine, and, wonderfully kind strangers. We put up a 1,000 posters. The Dog's Lost website and the kindness of others is what got me through. All I wanted was to be with Cassie, wherever she was. My heart had been ripped out.

Almost a week later, Cassie's body was found and retrieved by a very kind rail worker and collected by a pet crematorium. We never saw her but have her ashes, her collar and some fur.

Some time later, when I was more able to function, I began campaigning for this line to be fenced off in the park. The Rail company says the law is on their side; we say they are either breaking the law or the law needs to be changed.

Since then, I have volunteered to help others who have lost dogs. It's a constant reminder of my heartbreak and loss, but I have to do it as I understand only too well the pain of losing a dog.

Our vicar, Lynn, held a little service for our Cassie. She blessed her photo, her ashes and her fur. People say what happened was an accident, and from the human point of view, I suppose it was, but I know it was no accident. There were too many coincidences that night - even our friend, Annette, commented on that. The main one being how that train arrived at that precise second; the timing had to be exact, especially when there was only one, maybe two trains an hour at that time. What I saw and felt clearly told me it wasn't an accident. I believe this was something orchestrated by a higher power. I am still upset with God for taking her but I am sure that when I get to heaven He will explain why. Hopefully it will then all make sense.

Cassie was always such a special dog. I know all our dogs are special, each and every one of them, but there was something very special about Cassie - something different - and one of her middle names is Angel. She's now my angel until we are together again, properly this time, never to part ever again. Cassie truly earned her wings and I still miss her so much.

After losing Cassie in such a tragic way, my Mum and I were so looking forward to hearing from Cassie via Jackie. Due to my lack of hearing, our friend Annette took the call with Jackie for us. I was so excited but worried how I would understand everything. I need not have worried; Annette did a really great job and wrote everything down so I could read what Jackie was saying as she was saying it. Jackie would pause every so often to speak with Cassie before telling us what she was saying and Annette would be scribbling away.

First of all, Jackie said Cassie was jumping up and kissing me as she was so happy to be talking and had waited for this moment. I just sat there with tears pouring down my face, feeling sadness and happiness at the same time but barely able to speak, so it was a good job we had Annette doing the speaking anyway!

Cassie then described this funny thing like a scarf that goes around your neck; some kind of dog thing. Well, I didn't have a clue what that was despite Jackie describing it in more and more detail, best she could. But, whatever it was, Cassie thought it was really funny. So we kept it in mind.

Then Cassie told Jackie so many lovely things to relay to me. It meant so much and I will always keep this in my heart. Cassie was very busy in heaven acting as a guide, being here, there and everywhere, but she was always watching me too.

Everything she said about Cassie described her perfectly. Jackie said Cassie had her own confidence and would be fine staying in a room on her own. This was true. When we first got her, having been a rescue, she had separation anxiety so we worked through it, little by little and yes, she did very well. She would take herself off upstairs to have a snooze on our beds when she fancied. She felt secure, which is so lovely.

Jackie said Cassie was very intelligent - I can't explain how amazingly accurate that statement is. Cassie was (and still is) a very special dog. We had an amazing ability to communicate with each other and yes, as she told Jackie, she was able to guess what I was going to do before I did it. Before we'd go 'walkies' Cassie, of course, knew in advance and so we'd both be running about the house together getting leads, shoes, bag, treats, water etc. Sometimes, I'd forget something and we'd run up and down the stairs all over again.

Cassie told Jackie she laughs when watching me if I forget something, or go into a room and forget what I was getting. I couldn't help but be reminded of our running up and down the stairs ritual before we went out. Jackie said when you forget something, remember Cassie is watching you and laughing about it. Bless her.

Jackie said that Cassie smiles. She really did! She had the most beautiful, amazing eyes I've ever seen and she would smile - her whole face would light up and she would, well, smile. What Jackie said next, nearly knocked Annette off the chair, because Jackie said I kiss my fingers and put them on Cassie's photos and yes, I do, all the time. It was so lovely for me to know that Cassie watches me kiss her photos.

Jackie mentioned a couple of times about Cassie saying 'shake paws' and saying 'Hello, I'm here.' Such sweet memories - Cassie and I would sit together and she would put her paw out and I would hold it and then we'd have a cuddle. It was always our special moment together. But also, she would want to meet everyone who came in the house. If they didn't greet her she would go over and sit looking up at them, checking them out, until they said hello and 'shake paws' as Jackie put it! She was just like a human interacting.

Cassie also spoke of when I lost her and about the fence I was trying to get along the railway lines. Cassie said it was right for me to sort out the fence but not to let it consume my life. It had at that point, because I was so consumed with grief I didn't know what else to do with myself. She also said it will take a long time to go up and that it will drag on. This is what is happening. As I write this, it's been four and a half years since I lost my Cassie. I've been campaigning so hard and the local council and a member of Parliament are in agreement with fencing the track, but still the rail company does nothing. They have twice given assurances and twice changed their minds.

However, last year, I attended a council meeting. Cassie's Fence Campaign petition had at that time, about 7,000 signatures both on paper and online. I took 4,000 paper signatures from people using the park and showed them. I mentioned that a council officer who visited the site, had previously suggested that due to lack of assistance from the rail company, maybe the council could fence the pathway under the bridge where I lost my Cassie, as that was council land. I was met with some resistance from the officers present even though councillors and the MP had signed the petition! However, a few days later I was asked to meet officers on site. I thought I was going to have to fight for this fence and not being able to hear properly I got myself in such a state, I asked Jackie if she could sum up some 'heavenly' assistance. I knew I'd have my Cassie with me and Jackie sent some extra help in the form of her spirit guide, Rolf.

Amazingly, when I arrived I found I was not having to fight for a fence, but assisting in its location! It had already been agreed. I think it was the 4,000 signatures that helped! However, the chap from the council, who seemed to be acting under duress, clearly made it known he did not like dogs and felt quite hostile, but I knew I had 'Heaven' on my side.

We ended up, a month later, with a fence being erected on each side of the railway bridge! Although this was only a very small area of track accessibility, it was the most dangerous part where I lost my Cassie, and, as we found out later, where other dogs were getting access. Even though the rail company has yet to erect a continuous fence, as far as I'm concerned this small council fence is Cassie's Fence. We did it! She did it! She gave her life so others would live.

But, this is the not the end. Cassie's local Campaign will continue until the rail company in charge fences the whole track properly. Every now and then, I see a possibility that they are in fact listening, they just pretend they're not. A few weeks ago, I got word from the council that the rail company was commencing work to fence off the whole track! Could it be true this time? I live in hope, but still we wait... and I won't give up until it is done.

During Jackie's communication it was suggested we spread the Campaign further afield and that is exactly how the Campaign went! It has become National. Because of Cassie, other dog owners all around the country are becoming aware that this hidden danger exists. And, other owner's who have lost their dogs near a railway, now know to check, double check and triple check with the Rail authorities, even if the track appears fenced.

Sadly, many dogs have lost their lives to the railway and in parks without fencing. The only small consolation is that now many more owners can locate their beloved dogs and don't spend their lives searching and wondering where they are. But, they shouldn't lose their lives to a train in a park in the first place.

Jackie also mentioned that Cassie was saying another dog, elsewhere, had lost its life in the same way around the same time. Cassie gave the name 'Jack'. As yet we don't know any more, but perhaps one day we will. Jackie said I should do some voluntary work - that is exactly what I do now - I volunteer with DogLost.

Cassie showed Jackie us on our walks and Jackie said Cassie was a gentle soul as she was walking off lead, looking round checking on me and walking on and looking round checking again. We did have lovely walks and Cassie would usually be in front leading the way but always checking on me. She was my ears and my protector. Cassie knew I was struggling emotionally with her passing; she said there was a void. That void was the emptiness I felt without Cassie - I was still grieving. She told Jackie to tell me that she is safe and nothing is ever going to happen to her again. She also said what happened to her won't happen to Misty, our new rescue dog. I love Misty so much too and I panic if I can't see her on a walk because of what happened, but I rarely go to the river these days - it's just too hard. But Cassie was trying to help me; to reassure me. I am sure she watches over Misty, her new sister.

She also said I felt there was an injustice - that's true. I've always trusted in God but I couldn't understand why God would take Cassie from me knowing she was my world. Cassie said this "injustice" I felt was giving me strength that I didn't have before. Cassie also said she is always with me and when I'm missing her, I feel her next to me because she is there, saying "hello I'm here" and shaking paws, like she always did with me. She fills the room with sunshine and is giving me her smiley face. She wants me to be happy and positive. Cassie was also trying to tell me to believe in myself more. To have more self esteem. Jackie said Cassie was a 'higher being', an Angel on Earth. I always knew she was extra special and this confirmed it. She also said she was sent to earth for a purpose and it was her time to go. She said it was a freak accident and not to blame myself because there was nothing I could have done to prevent it - it was meant to be. As hard as that is, I do know, deep inside. I felt it was taken out of my hands; events were unfolding and I was powerless to stop it. It was an awful feeling but in another way, it does prove to me that there is more to this life than we know.

Jackie said of all the dogs we could have got, we found Cassie - we were together for a reason. I know I will be with Cassie again one day and I know the reason is our love.

Jackie made us laugh, when she asked if we gave Cassie some dinner from our plates because she can see her eyes following the food asking if its for her! I know exactly what that was. Occasionally, my Mum and I would have a snack of cheese and crackers in front of the TV. After we first got Cassie and she was sitting with us, I noticed she was watching the food intently as I picked up the crackers and then the cheese and put them together. I then deliberately moved the food sideways and up and down to see if that is what she was actually doing. And yes! She followed the food in my hand with her eyes no matter where I moved it. She was so funny. Once I realised, I never made deliberate movements again but she always followed the cheese and I always gave her some. So yes, it was for her! It is little things like this that make you know spirit life is real and able to bring back lovely memories to cherish, always.

Cassie signed off by saying, 'I was an angel on Earth and you are a far better person than you think. I loved you and still do." She was very specific about the words - they mean so much to me. Thank you my baby, I loved you and still do. Every time I re-read Cassie's chat via Jackie, it means more each time. I am so grateful to Jackie for doing this and for my Cassie's loving words that I keep with me until we are reunited again in heaven and can speak in person.

Oh, and that funny scarf affair that we couldn't place at the start? When the conversation ended and Jackie had gone, our friend Annette said, "You know I have a feeling that was to do with me". I asked why she didn't say anything, but it seemed she was so blown away by it all she couldn't believe Cassie would be talking about her as well! It turned out that Cassie had been watching Annette try on this novelty 'dog' neck warmer that she was thinking of buying me for Christmas! Cassie thought it was hilarious and was letting Annette know that she knew about it too.

**

So maybe you think the story ends there and Kim is still watching and waiting. Well, how is this for a bit of spiritual synchronicity... Kim could have sent me her story anytime but timing is timing. Whilst I was checking her story this end, the rail company were actually fencing at her end!! And, not just on one side but both sides! Her local Essex newspaper ran the story, complete with a photo of Kim holding up a placard with Cassie's photo on it saying VICTORY! To make this 'victory' complete, please, please, if you know of any lengths of rail track that are not fenced off and are a danger to animals etc. complain to your local rail company. We should not have to put up with needless deaths and I know that Kim, and Cassie, will help you, should you need it, too.

*****

Revelations from Heaven...

Kelly and her Mum - their cat Marmite

Marmite was a special cat. I knew that from the first moment I saw him when he was a kitten. I used to babysit for the family he lived with and our bond grew stronger with each visit. One night as I stayed over and Marmite crept into bed with me for cuddles, I really wished that he lived with me. Imagine my surprise as my wish came true! When Marmite was a year old, the lady couldn't look after him anymore so he came to live with my mum and I. Marmite was delighted to be part of our family - together at last, we had so many happy times. He was such a clever, affectionate and funny cat - always making us laugh, I loved him so much.

When Marmite reached nine years old, he started to get problems with his waterworks and passing blood whenever he went to the toilet. We took him to the vets and they said he had a blockage and required a special diet but that was all. In hindsight, I should have asked for further tests but I just accepted what they said. Afterwards, he seemed to get better until about seven months later when he started to have a bit of trouble eating which I thought was down to dental problems. My mum and I had a trip booked in May to visit a relative who we don't get to see often - we actually thought about cancelling the visit and take Marmite back to the vets instead but, as I honestly didn't think for one minute anything serious was wrong with him, we arranged to take him after we returned a week later.

The day we returned my aunt, who had been looking after him, seemed worried. Marmite was having difficulty breathing and hadn't eaten anything. We took him straight to the vets and my worst ever fear was realised. The vet told us he had a tumour in his abdomen that had spread. Further tests showed it was cancerous and had spread so much there was no hope. We had his lungs drained to help him breathe and some medicine to help him eat and arranged for him to be put to sleep at home. My world fell apart. On 21st May 2013, as Marmite who had just turned ten years old, fell asleep in my arms. When he died a part of me died too. My mum and I buried him in a beautiful coffin with roses printed on it under his favourite tree in the garden.

A few weeks later I was visiting a pet bereavement website when one forum post in particular caught my eye. A lady whose dog had died, mentioned a spirit communication with Jackie and I read about in amazement. There and then, I decided to give it a go and sent an email to Jackie. We arranged a communication via webcam and I wasn't sure what to expect but, from the very start, Jackie was lovely and made me feel at ease.

The first thing she said to me was that Marmite was telling her about the trouble with his kidneys and I knew straight away it was him. I felt overwhelmed with emotion. Jackie described Marmite as being soft and cuddly which was very true; I used to call him my baby panda because of his lovely thick, soft fur. She also said he loved his comforts and his bed, also very true and how his face used to be close to mine; he used to sleep with me, very close and I always used to kiss him on the head.

I told Jackie I felt guilty for not spotting signs of his illness sooner and for going away and she said I wasn't to feel guilty as Marmite told her his kidneys wouldn't have been strong enough to cope with chemotherapy anyway. I hadn't thought of it like that and that gave me such a sense of relief. I also knew he didn't like going to the vets or having to leave home.

I was blown away when Jackie repeated to me things that my mum and I had said just before Marmite died. She also said it had taken a while for Marmite to adjust to being in Heaven but that he had friends there and, in particular, an elderly lady. Marmite was always a ladies cat; he had two women who lived around the corner from us that he used to visit everyday. One of them has lots of cats that he used to enjoy playing with. It was this part of Marmite's "secret life" that I discovered through the communication with Jackie, it was as if he wanted me and mum to know about what he got up to.

Amongst other things he described being on top of a structure and looking down through it. I had no idea what he was referring to so thought nothing more about it until, after speaking with the ladies who were asking why they hadn't seen Marmite, I discovered one of them had a conservatory that Marmite used to climb up on to and look through it at them! He also described his cat friends – who we didn't know but afterwards started to visit us, and still do. It was funny how little things Jackie said that didn't mean anything at the time came to light much later, I know Marmite would have been smiling down as each little revelation became apparent.

His personality really came across during the communication and he made us laugh. He tickled us when he described my mum running out in the rain to the clothes line to grab the washing in whilst he watched her urgency through the patio door - it seemed to amuse him greatly. Towards the end of our communication, Jackie told me that Marmite was referring to a silver photo frame with a picture of him in it. This was significant because we had placed a candle in front of it to light after he passed away. He told Jackie he would like his name engraved on it, so that's what I did.

Jackie told us so many things about Marmite that no one but our family could have known. We laughed and cried and the communication helped with the grieving process. To know that Marmite is not lonely in the spirit world is a real comfort. We miss Marmite so much; he was such a wonderful companion but now when I shed a tear, I can also smile thinking of our conversation with Jackie.

I thank Jackie for the lovely reading with Marmite, she is such a kind and gifted person, I would recommend this experience to anyone.

*****

Whilst losing one love but gaining another…

Giuseppe and his cat Nini

Nini had just passed away in my arms. The pain of losing my darling black and white boy after his long illness, was unbearable. He was old but was so strong and fought so hard, it destroyed a part of me forever. Life was supposed to be happy, I was soon to be a father. I held Nini in my arms whilst the vet gave him his final injection, and, as I looked up at the photograph of the 30-week-scan of our son-to-be, my Nini passed away.

I called for my father in law to help me and while we both sat in our house's boot-room we both heard three loud knocks on the door. We both said, 'Come in, come in' but nobody appeared! I knew who it was... my Nini had come back in Spirit, away from the vets car and back to me once more. I felt the blackness of my pain become lighter and felt the pain felt less intense. It was still there, but I could deal with it.

That was the 29th of January 2014 and from then on, I then started making notes of the signs Nini left for me to show me that he was still alive in Spirit and with me sometimes too.

In February, Grayson my first child was due to be born and having also moved permanently from London to our new home in the North of England, I was barely recovering from the intensity of that when I lost my adored and best friend Nini.

I had booked my phone call with Jackie a few weeks before Grayson was born which actually turned out to be the day after his birth. So, after spending my first full day with my wife and son, I ended up taking the call at the back of the canteen, as I didn't want to miss out on speaking to my darling cat. I cried in that canteen. It all hit me - the loss of Nini, the depth of becoming a new father. I was grieving for Nini but was also rejoicing having been graced and blessed with our absolutely gorgeous son, Grayson. A hugely emotional time of my life to say the least.

I knew Jackie would tell me about Nini, and I knew that she would be my new link with him and she most certainly was. Yes, of course I live with doubt, as do many religious people, as mediumship is certainly not what goes with our belief. Doubt comes at the dark times, but my belief is that Nini is with me and, thanks to Jackie, I also believe that he is happy and free from the pain of his body and illness.

When Jackie spoke to me at the hospital I was in the most disorganised state I have ever been! I am incredibly 'OCD' (obsessive compulsive disorder) and organised, well I was before Grayson came into our lives. I didn't take any notes of what she said, but wrote them down afterwards as best as I could. 'Gentle Boy' is the first thing that Nini told Jackie to tell me. Yes he was; he was a noble and deep soul. Gentle is a good way to say that Nini was my Rock. Just like a rock, he was gently keeping my life anchored without ever upsetting me. Jackie shared many more aspects of our life together, and the depth of our relationship shone through. She said he was like a little person to me and I couldn't agree more.

Nini said I seemed to have been 'spotting' rainbows since he had gone. This was so true. To be honest, I had not paid much attention to them before but I am sure he was pointing them out to me as another sign from him. The day after the reading, whilst walking our dogs, a magnificent one appeared, so I took a photo and emailed it straight to Jackie.

I was so surprised when Nini shared some work advice about some buildings which, amazingly, my father and myself had only looked at the day before! I was so pleased to know that Nini is watching me, and am sure over Grayson too.

I still miss and think about Nini everyday, but I can only hope to meet up with my boy again when I pass to the afterlife too.

*****

Truly Heaven sent...

Kirsty and her cat Humphrey

In June 2013 I was driving my friend to the railway station after a fantastic weekend catching-up, when we came across a horrific accident in which a motorcyclist had collided with a car. The motorcyclist was in a really bad way - unconscious, broken neck, broken limbs and signs of a brain injury and internal bleeding. Despite my friend's and my best efforts at CPR both on our own and then alongside the paramedics, he died whilst we were with him. I had witnessed death before (I work in the healthcare profession) but never in someone so young and never outside a 'clinical' environment. It deeply affected me. I couldn't eat, I couldn't sleep. I kept getting flashbacks. Even though the paramedics had said his injuries were so severe that there was nothing anyone could have done to save him, I felt that somehow I had let this person down. I ended up speaking to a psychologist friend, and he gently suggested I seek support for PTSD. Although I did a lot of yoga and meditation during this time I didn't want to speak to a professional as all I could think was, "I just wish I could go back and do things differently. I wish I could save him"

Six weeks later (to the hour) I was driving home, about a mile away from where the accident had been. I was running late to meet a friend but rather than taking my usual, direct route, I chose to divert along a little side street, which I rarely use because it is further and slower. I can't explain why I did this; there was no obvious reason, I just did. In the middle of the road was a little bundle of tabby and white fur. Other cars were slowing and driving around it. I pulled over and raced over to check if the bundle was alive. As soon as I got closer I realised it was a male cat - alive but barely conscious and lying in his own urine and faeces. I moved him to the side of the road and placed him on the pavement but he just fell over straight away. I tried to find someone to ask if they knew who he was but no-one was around so I bundled him in the car and took him to our local veterinarian.

The vet examined him and he was in a really bad way - he was very underweight, had a really large mass in his abdomen, a severe flea infestation causing anaemia, a systemic infection, arthritis in his back legs, rotting teeth and abscesses so bad that he had osteomyelitis (bone infection) in his jaw. Blood tests also showed problems with his liver and kidneys. He was also very elderly, completely deaf and absolutely filthy. Despite all this, he was so calm and purred the entire time - just seemingly grateful for any small act of kindness and affection. The vet explained to us that the prognosis was very poor, that he was close to death and that in the circumstances it may be kindest to euthanise him there and then. We asked if we could take him home for the night and armed with flea treatments and antibiotics off we went. Once home we treated him for fleas, fed him (he was starving), started the antibiotics, gave him fresh water and even bathed him - he purred the whole time! He spent the evening on the sofa with my husband and me, just sleeping and purring.

Although I've always loved animals and nursed lots of strays in the past I felt such a strong and immediate connection to Humphrey (yes, we named him almost straight away and the name just really suited him!) and I made a vow to him there and then I would do anything I could to give him a happy and peaceful end to his life, even if that was only for a few days.

Over the next few days Humphrey went from strength to strength. Each day he was a little stronger and a little healthier. After a month he was doing so well that the vet felt he would be able to go through a general anaesthetic to remove the infected teeth. We had a nail-biting day waiting to hear from them but he sailed through the op and after more antibiotics for the abscesses and osteomyelitis he made even more improvements to his health. He continued to improve for another eight months.

From day one he just settled in. He learned how to use a litter tray and he settled into a very happy routine of feeds, cuddles, playtime, more feeds, sitting and watching the world go by out of the big bay window from his sofa.... Both my husband and I fell in love with him almost instantly. We had never met a cat so affectionate, so loving, so characterful in his facial expressions and so trusting, especially after what he had been through.

All of our friends and family fell for him too, even

those who profess not to like cats! During his frequent visits to the vet he was greeted like a celebrity by all the staff who repeatedly referred to him as their "favourite patient". The vet herself could hardly believe how well he was doing. Each time she examined him she would shake her head, consider his innumerable health problems and say, "Well, despite all the odds he seems to be doing really well". To begin with we would take him to the vet in a pet carrier, but it seems this was the one thing he didn't like, as he would yowl constantly. After we got to know him a little better though, we realised that he was as good as gold just sitting on my knee in the car whilst my husband drove us. He would just sit there looking out of the window with fascination, purring constantly. He was so happy in the car that we even started taking him with us to visit friends and to dinner parties! He would have his own food bowl, water bowl and litter tray with him and once he knew where these things were he would settle down on the sofa and sleep, occasionally opening his eyes just long enough to check that we were still nearby!

During this time we repeatedly tried to find Humphrey's 'owner' but with no luck. He wasn't micro-chipped and despite our best attempts via the Internet and putting posters up, nobody ever came forward.

My husband and I live in a top floor flat in the city, with two free-range, rescued budgies. We always assumed that we wouldn't be able to have a cat whilst we were here but Humphrey just took to it straight away. He was always fascinated by the budgies and once made a leap at them - my husband picked him up and put him in the kitchen on his own for a few minutes. I joked at the time that he was wasting his time as you couldn't train a cat not to chase birds but after this he never tried to approach them again, and instead watched their antics quietly from his spot on the sofa.

I was very keen that Humphrey could have access to the outdoors if he wanted it so I bought him a harness. We would frequently go down to the communal garden, have a wander round or just sit in the sun. Once he had had enough he would look at me, get up and wander back to the front door to go inside. We soon dispensed with the harness and would just spend a sunny afternoon outside together until he was ready and would give me the sign to go back indoors. During these few months we lost our 24-year-old family cat, Mitzy, who was living with my mum and dad. Unlike Humphrey who, despite our encouragement, was not happy being on our bed and would only ever sleep on his sofa, Mitzy always used to sleep on the bed with my mum, usually lying on her chest with her paws on my mum's face. If my mum wasn't at home she would sleep like this on the next available person! The night before Mitzy passed away I was lying in bed reading when Humphrey came into the room, jumped on the bed and came and lay on my chest with his paws on my face. He stayed like that until I fell asleep. He had never done this before and never did it again. It felt like Mitzy somehow saying goodbye.

Things were going so well, despite all his persistent health issues that we really started to believe that he would last for another few months, maybe even another few years. However, in May of this year he suddenly went downhill. He stopped eating and became very weak. In desperation, we bought in as much tempting food as we could think of - raw liver, smoked salmon, dressed crab, beef stew, steak.... and we hand-fed him. (We don't eat meat or indeed any other animal products so these treats were purely for him!) We willed him to pull through. He started eating again and for a few days we thought we'd cracked it then he would stop eating again. This happened three or four times over the next month. Eventually it got to the point where no amount of love, veterinary care and TLC was enough. The mass in his abdomen was getting bigger and due to his age and health problems none of us felt it was fair to put him through invasive and painful surgery. He had completely stopped eating, was barely drinking and went off his legs. We had to make the heart-breaking decision to put him to sleep. We arranged for the vet to come to our home the following morning and, despite the overwhelming heartache we vowed to try to make his last night as special and as comfortable as possible. We both stayed in the lounge with him all night, cuddling him, telling him how much we loved him, how special he was to us, what a difference he had made to our lives... We watched the sun come up together on that final morning. We managed to stay reasonably strong until the vet had given him that final injection and then we both just fell apart. The next few days and weeks were horrendous. We both cried so much and despite our best efforts to comfort each other we were just so completely consumed by our grief and the unbelievable sense of loss.

I've always been a strong, and often conflicting, mix of practical and spiritual. I have a science degree so it's completely ingrained in me that I need "proof" for everything. However, since being young I have seen "ghosts" on more than one occasion, often get a strong sense of the "feel" of places, especially in places that turn out to have a traumatic past and have often had a strong sense that something is going to happen, before it does. After we lost Humphrey I was desperate for a sign that he still existed in some way, that he was ok and that we had made the right decision at the end. I asked him for a sign - I kept seeing rainbows, even indoors where I had never seen them before, I picked up a pack of Oracle cards (they were given to me by a friend and I had never used them before) and asked him for a sign - I repeatedly picked out a card that said "your loved ones are safe in heaven". I even, on a long motorway journey one day, asked him for a green lorry to show me he was ok - for the next ten minutes every single lorry I saw was green. (Yes, grief makes you a little crazy!) Despite all of this I remained cynical, dismissing everything as pure coincidence, of my grieving mind trying to find some comfort, and kept most of it to myself.

Still struggling with my grief I came across a book about animals and the afterlife written by an American author. It was an enormous comfort and started to make me think there may be "something else". It mentioned animal communication, which I had never heard of before. I Googled and found Jackie's details. I was still incredibly sceptical but figured I couldn't feel any worse than I did already. I emailed Jackie and provided her just with my name, Humphrey's name and a photograph of him. I deliberately didn't give her any extra information as I felt that I needed to "test" her if I was going to gain any real comfort from the session. Jackie carried out a telephone consultation a week later, which she described as a "three way conversation" between me, her and Humphrey.

As soon as Jackie came on the 'phone she explained

that as soon as she had contacted Humphrey she had had an overwhelming feeling of being "full", of there being something inside her, of nausea, of something pressing on her stomach and of feeling that she wanted to eat but she couldn't. This described Humphrey's symptoms to the letter.

Over the next 40 minutes more and more information followed that Jackie just couldn't have known - she described how he had been living as a stray before we found him, that he had only been with us for a short time but that he felt "like he had come home" and settled in straight away. She said she felt that Humphrey had passed away after an illness but went very suddenly at the end.

She described what my husband does for a job, details of the layout of the flat, things that Humphrey liked to do. She even said that he was showing her Oracle cards that I had been using to try and communicate with him (no-one knew this, not even my friends and family!)

She went on to explain that Humphrey had come into my life for a very specific reason. At this point I said that there had been an accident a few weeks beforehand. Jackie said that Humphrey wanted me to know that there was nothing else I could have done and that it was the man's "time to go". He also explained that he had been my "angel". I had always called him "Angel" but again, Jackie didn't know this. I had goosebumps several times during the conversation and by the end had a feeling of reassurance, comfort and peace that I hadn't felt in a long time.

Since my conversation with Jackie I have spoken to a few friends about it and been greeted by a mixed response - some people being totally fascinated and open to the idea and others completely cynical. The fact is that things came out of that conversation that Jackie just couldn't have known or deduced.

Of course I still miss Humphrey every single day; I still feel that a part of me is missing and I'm crying whilst I type this but I also feel that he IS still out there and that he's watching over me and that is incredibly reassuring.

Thank you Jackie.

****

Some divine intervention to get her owners to the right place, at the right time so she could speak...

Gloria and Pete's dog Candy

We were going dog training with our dog Lucy, a Collie x Spaniel, when we met a lady there who was training her King Charles Cavalier. We fell in love this type of little dog and decided we would look around and see if there were any puppies for sale.

I found one but when I phoned she said they were all gone but another litter was nearly ready to leave soon. We were over the moon and said we would have a ruby coloured girl. We didn't see her until we went to collect her and it turned out she was at a puppy farm. I didn't realise this and, as wrong as they are, we could not then walk away and leave her there.

We loved her as soon as we saw her; she was such a sweetie so we called her Candy. The day after we had her we had to rush her to the vet. She was very poorly (sadly typical of farmed puppies who often do not get the correct dietary needs and proper attention) and the vets said the next 24 hours were touch and go. We couldn't believe that this little bundle of joy could leave us. We cuddled her all night. Thankfully she turned the corner and recovered. She had the odd flare-ups of the colitis from time to time, but we managed it.

Candy was very much top dog, and with us too I think. She was a proper lady. She wouldn't jump in and out of our car; we had to lift her. If something was in her way she wouldn't jump over it; we had to move it! We went obedience training with her and she got her bronze, silver and gold.

When she was two years old, she had a Pyometra - a severely infected womb and life threatening. She was very poorly and had an emergency operation to remove it. As always she bounced back.

At five years old she wasn't quite herself but we didn't know what it was, but felt something was wrong. I just kept telling the vets that something wasn't right with her so in the end they referred us to a specialist vet for scans. They found out she had bladder stones but also she had problem with her kidneys too. Unbelievably, they said she only had about a year to live. We were heart broken but, with treatment, she was her usual self.

We used to call her 'Kick Ass Lil' as she was such a little toughie - whatever came her way, she fought and survived, we prayed that this would also be the case again. She was such a character and enjoyed our caravan holidays. She was not a lover of too much walking but she always go for a wander with my husband Pete. Ten months before her passing we got another puppy and he got so attached to her, and her to him. She played with him, which was surprising as she had never done with any of the others. She became his mum. She always put him in his place. The weekend of her passing she wasn't well and we knew that on the Monday we would be at the vets. We cuddled her all weekend and the other dogs lay with her - they knew too.

When we arrived at the vets, they confirmed her kidneys were giving up; she was in renal failure. We had to say goodbye to her and told her we loved her right to her last breath. We miss her so very much; she was so very special and will always be in our hearts and home.

We knew there was a big holistic festival coming up so we decided (for some unknown reason) that we should go along. Whilst there, I spotted a sign for an Animal Communication Workshop by Jackie Weaver 'The Animal Psychic'. I was intrigued, so I went and I have to say, I truly enjoyed it and realised, maybe this was the reason we wanted to come. Afterwards we went into the main arena and saw Jackie was there doing readings. I hung around and waited to see her as I wanted to ask if she would connect with Candy for us. She smiled and said for me, and my husband, to sit down and asked for the limited details that she had explained about in the workshop.

Jackie connected straight away and Candy said that we still had her bed. Yes, we did! Jackie had to tell me to write down what she was saying as I would not remember all that was said and could refer back to it later if I wanted to. I am so glad I did, which is how I can write my story for this book and read my notes whenever I need a 'Candy moment' too.

Candy also said about the washing machine breaking and water all over the floor! How funny that I should now be happy about such an annoyance, but it happened since her passing, so I know she is still watching over us. Candy said she also liked being top dog and that she was never any trouble, unlike the others (somehow we ended up four) and that was so true! She was bossy, but in a good way, and never gave us an ounce of trouble in the seven wonderful years we had her. She explained to Jackie that, when they were all going out, the others would run out of the door together but she would walk out to the car in her own time then waited to be lifted in! There was so much laughter with that connection.

We have got another pup now which we are sure was hand-picked by Candy herself. She has got Candy's markings of white on her chin and paws and we are certain she's got plenty of Candy's personality in her too.

Candy even told Jackie that it was beautiful there (Heaven) and we will love it when we get there too. We are so very thankful to Jackie for the connection. We know that they live on and watch over us. We will love you always Candy.

*****

This is Sid who 'jumped in' on his friend Josh's communication...

Andy and Karen's horse Sid

This is every horse owner's nightmare...it is 2am and you have been trying for hours to save your horse from an impaction colic and nothing is working. He is in too much pain to travel and the vet is asking you to make that awful heart-breaking decision. With a heavy heart we decided to let Sid go as there was nothing more that we could do for him.

In the end we were thankful it happened at home, so our other horse, Josh could see Sid's body afterwards and start his grieving process too. They have lived together, just the two of them, for eight years and Josh was not taking it well. We decided to take him to a friend's yard to see if company would help but after being there all day, he didn't settle and we were getting so worried about him, we brought him back home again.

In panic I phoned Jackie for some guidance, as she had spoken to Josh before and I wanted to find out what he was thinking. While waiting on a pony friend to be delivered from a family member, Jackie called me back.

First I felt a huge sense of relief to speak to her. She said that Josh wanted to be home with us and not in a strange place; he wanted to keep an eye on us as we were so upset too.

Jackie then started talking about Sid. She hadn't spoken to Sid before, had no details or photo of him, so this was quite unexpected. Firstly she said he is fine, and that he wanted me to know he is in a field at the top of a hill and the large flock of sheep who were waiting for him. 'Oh My God!' were my exact words. When we bought him eight years previously, he had been one horse living in a field full of sheep! On the day we went to collect him, he was lying down in the field surrounded by 'his sheep'. I cannot recall him being near any sheep since then. Wow.

Jackie she said he told her the way he would pass was a long time coming and that I would understand that. YES I completely understand. Poor Sid had been suffering from gas colic for about two years and had been particularly bad at the beginning of that year. Vet investigations could not find anything that was causing it. These gas colic episodes were very frequent but quite mild. Something in his body just didn't work properly!

It was a brief call, as I was too upset to do much more but it gave me a huge sense of peace that he was happy and no longer in pain. My heart was eased that Josh understood what was going on, and that we were right to bring him home. We knew we would miss Sid as much as we do but, whenever we see a flock of sheep, they now hold a whole new meaning to us.

Thank you Jackie for being there in my time of need.

*****

A golden ray of sunshine…

Ian and his Dog Alfie

I had just recovered from a long illness back in 2005 and my two children were desperate for a dog and having had dogs in my childhood, secretly so was I. My wife's father had recently lost their Golden Retriever, Scott, and as he was an excellent family dog so we decided to opt for the same breed.

We picked up our puppy, Alfie, in time for him to share his first Christmas with us, his new family. The breeder said she knew he would be all right with us as she described how her heart melted as she looked at my daughter's face as Alfie was handed over.

He grew up to be a great dog and was not only loved by us but by virtually anyone whose path he crossed. He was a favourite with friends and neighbours and people who he met on his walks. He was prone to going into strangers houses who had left their door open to have a look round for food. He would regularly follow the postman around on his walk around our cul-de-sac. He liked to be wherever we were and was happy chewing a stick as he watched me working in the garden or washing my car. He just loved being with us. He had Colitis on and off over the years and was treated for the odd limp and we thought in our minds that perhaps his hips may be his undoing in old age.

My wife, who wasn't that fussed about having a dog, fell totally in love with him as much as we did. We got so much pleasure from him over the years - he was a great 'stress buster' and the exercise was great for the whole family too. Alfie loved the car and the sight of his car blanket and lead bought great excitement. He enjoyed walks most in the countryside where he went most, if not all, days. He was very friendly towards cats - some would let him come close and even sniff them as long as he wasn't over enthusiastic in his approach. He was a big softy with a beautiful cream coat. He loved chewing sticks in the garden and there were regular comical attempts at him trying to get a large stick through our narrow back gate.

Once his eighth birthday had passed, Alfie started to slow down on his walks and panted more than usual. We took him to the vets, which was yet another place he enjoyed! There was a suspicion that his colitis had flared up again. He seemed to pick up but then went off his food. The vet suggested X-rays but, within the space of a few days, Alfie stopped going out for walks and lay in strange places in the house. He began to groan whenever he moved and we were getting terribly concerned. He had pain-killing injections but to no avail and my wife slept down stairs with him for three nights. He was urgently referred to a specialist vet and the X-rays confirmed cancer in his lymph nodes and lungs that had most probably spread from a primary site somewhere else. I knew in my heart that he was really poorly. He was only eight-years-old so we were devastated by the diagnosis and inevitable conclusion that nothing could be done for him.

We had to make the most difficult decision, there and then, that the kindest thing would be to put Alfie to sleep. We obviously stayed with him for what was a surreal experience as, in truth, he had only been really poorly for a few days. He was still the big old softy, tail wagging and to look at him, you would have not have guessed he was so ill. However, his tail wagging was only a show for the vet, so typical of him. We lost our beautiful boy and friends and neighbours were also devastated. We received sixteen sympathy cards, flowers and plants from people around us who shared in our loss.

We all found it difficult to accept the loss of Alfie and looked for a sign that he might still be around or would let us know that he was ok. This never came so via the internet, I was drawn to Jackie Weaver having seen her in newspapers and on TV and wondered if she could help us through this terrible grief.

Shortly before the agreed telephone reading it went very dark outside and began to thunder. It quickly brightened up as Jackie telephoned. I had a slide show of Alfie running on the PC and his ashes by me.

Jackie put me at my ease and informed me that Alfie was at peace and was thankful for our efforts with his health. She knew that his loss resulted from problems with his breathing and made reference to problems with his back legs too. He had a tumour that was causing lameness in his back legs that only became evident in his last 24 hours.

Jackie cheered us up by referring to the fact that Alfie was not resting in peace (a term I do not like) but resting in Party! He was feeling rejuvenated and having time of his life but was keeping a watchful eye on us in all that we did. She referred to his love of cars and his special car blanket. She also mentioned that Alfie said he would 'lick a cat' which was reference to his fondness of cats.

She also said Alfie had been sent to me as a Guardian Angel after my ill health and that sadly, sometimes guardians get called back at younger years, hence his loss at just eight. He told Jackie that I felt cheated, and I did. Through Jackie he said, 'No, you had eight great years with me and I was grateful for the time I had with you.'

I asked if dogs have a Heaven and she said of course they do, and with humans too! She told me Alfie was with a man that had a pronounced limp and immediately I thought of my wife's father – he did have a limp! My wife burst into tears when I told her, as we now knew Alfie was in good hands.

Jackie also said Alfie liked to chase a frisbee down a hill but I told her that he preferred to chase big stones on his walks. At first I did not understand the reference to a hill but then realised his favourite walk was called Withy Hill! That is where he chased the stones down the hill and I realised he did have a frisbee in his younger days which probably would have been better for his teeth than his chosen stones! She also made reference to a dogs name Poppy; although Alfie had a Labrador friend called Poppy, we saw more relevance in the fact that, our first time on Withy Hill since losing Alfie, the walk was lined with masses of poppies.

Jackie also mentioned Alfie's love of wooded areas, which was true, and that another of his favourite walks which seemed to have three ponds. It took me a minute to place this area but then quickly realised it was Alfie's Green Man walk. He loved to watch as I chucked stones into the water – how I miss such simple things we did together.

In his last few days, the smoke detector's low battery warning beep started to go off and we all hated the irritating noise that, for some reason, always started in the middle of the night. Not long after Alfie's passing, the second smoke detector then started to beep in the middle of the night too! We thought was quite unusual and perhaps Alfie was just letting us know that he was still about and happy to wake us up as he did with his barking from time to time.

There were so many things that the wonderfully gifted Jackie was able to tell us about Alfie that no one else would have known. It was a great relief to talk to her and from her reading realise that Alfie was doing great and was keeping a watchful eye out for us. After all, he was, and still is, our Guardian Angel. Alfie said he would not object to us having another Golden Retriever and indeed, we hope that just a little bit of his spirit would follow any new puppy we might have in the future. Having had eight such amazing years with Alfie, we could not see ourselves (even now the children are grown up) not sharing our lives with such a wonderful canine companion.

I can recall a saying that goes... There is a single lady in our village looking for a male friend. I ask her if she fancied a companion who was: handsome, affectionate, snug in bed, devoted to her, loyal, protective and seeking only to please? She replies, 'Yes, that was exactly what I had in mind!' and I reply, 'Then I would warmly recommend you get a Golden Retriever!' That says it all!

*****

Loving is giving...

Bev and her dog Gilly

Gilly came to me at the tender age of six weeks old as I was a puppy walker for Guide Dogs for the Blind. She was a beautiful yellow Golden Retriever/Labrador cross and being a guide dog puppy she could have gone to anyone but her carers had desperately wanted her to come to me. She was so small and fragile and looked just like her mum who I had also puppy walked several years before. Gilly had got stuck in the birth canal and had fought to survive, but survive she did. I called her my Angel right from the very start; she was such a special little girl.

After having her for only 24 hours, she started to pass large amounts of blood in her urine. The vet thought it was a possible kidney problem, and things looked rather bleak. She was returned to the breeding centre to be looked after and we were told that she may not return to us. But after three weeks, and several types of antibiotics to clear up a nasty case of cystitis, she did come back home to us.

It was clear from the very start that Gilly had severe hip dysplasia and her hips would pop in and out of their sockets. She didn't like walking along pavements with cars approaching from behind her; she would go into complete shut-down. Gilly was not destined to be a guide dog, and she was put up for adoption. Guide Dogs have a waiting list of families wishing to take on pups that are not suitable. There were no takers as no one wanted a little pup with horrendous hips who wouldn't walk but I did! The only dilemma was, we already had two Golden Retrievers, and I wished to puppy walk again so four dogs would have been too many. Then disaster struck, in a cruel twist of fate, I unexpectedly lost my youngest Goldie, Tilly. Of course Gilly stayed, where she had belonged all the time, with me. She was a very gentle little soul who adored everything and everyone.

Due to the state of her hips she needed hydrotherapy. Pam, an amazing lady, who ran the pool was very supportive to both Gilly and me. She introduced me to Canine Health Concern. I was made aware of the need to feed an appropriate raw diet, stop the over use of vaccination and replace chemical wormers and flea treatments with natural products. Gilly bloomed into an even more beautiful little girl, and her confidence grew.

On Christmas Eve in 2013 I noticed that Gilly had blood in her urine. I wasn't overly concerned, but managed to get her an appointment that evening with my vet. Antibiotics were prescribed. The bleeding continued well into the New Year. Eventually, a kidney scan and the insertion of a endoscopic camera diagnosed an idiopathic renal haemorrhage. (Idiopathic meaning a condition that appears with no medical reason.) This was very rare and with no known treatment. She was fine until March until she became very unwell, a further scan showed that her kidneys had changed shape and I had to prepare that our time together was running out. Her Spondylitis (a condition that affects the spine) which had also become apparent a few years earlier had also reared it's ugly head, making life difficult.

I had to let my sweet girl go to be with the Angels on the 26th April 2014 at just seven years old. My heart was truly broken. Through her I have met some amazing people, made some special friends and been introduced to natural health care for my dogs and help share this information with others. She taught me that while you can be gentle and fragile, you can also be sturdy and strong. I feel truly blessed to have shared seven years of my life with such a special little girl.

In July 2014, I went to The Healing Weekend in Somerset. This was a massive festival with psychic readers, healers, musicians, artists and the list goes on. Anything positive and good for your soul, you could find it there. As I was walking around I spotted Jackie, I was drawn to her. I told her that she had looked a nice lady, she laughed.

I asked if she could connect with Gilly. When she said that she was soft and gentle I knew that she had her. She said that she felt a pain in her stomach and that Gilly had started to pick up during her illness and then went downhill again, which was correct. She said that there had been a problem with her right hip, but it had not stopped her from playing and doing what she had wanted to do, which was completely right. She showed Jackie lots of flowers. I explained that when she had passed I received many flowers, plants and cards and that I had placed them all together with a picture of Gilly in the centre. Jackie asked if Gilly had a teddy bear - lots of them I said. Gilly said that my other dog doesn't always listen, how true was that! She said that I'm not to worry about her as she will be okay.

Gilly thought that she would like a charity named after her and I replied, "Trust her, how am I supposed to do that?" Jackie asked Gilly and said, "Giving is Loving." What beautiful words and smiled at the suggestion of that being a wonderful charity slogan. Perhaps one day Gilly, perhaps. She said that there were exciting times ahead for me. She also said that I have a lot of knowledge and I must not always bite my tongue and let others do all the talking. I will try.

Jackie also said that I would meet a cheeky tri-coloured Jack Russell, complete with a long tail. Well, last week I certainly did meet him! A friend of mine had fostered him but decided to adopt him. I had goosebumps when I knelt down to say hello to him. I know it was Gilly's confirmation of my reading.

At the end of the reading, I purchased one of Jackie's books, which I asked her to sign. She added a message from Gilly, and it read, 'To mum, love is eternal, speak for me.' Thank you Jackie, you were amazing.

*****

Postscript

I thank each and every one of you for sharing your beautiful stories in this book. Bless you for trusting me to connect with your animal and, of course Stan and Rolf (my other guide) for bringing them forward to talk with you once again.

I am honoured to do what I do and help make a difference to people's lives. Having let people know this book was on its way, more people have come forward with their stories too! So, if you are reading this, and I have done a spirit communication for you, please let me know if you want your reading to be in the next book as well.

A huge thank you to Joy, Neshla and Monica for their wonderful pre-checking, pro-editing and post-checking. Thank you ladies. Also, a special mention for my wonderful friend Beth who passed on Stan's message about writing this book.

If you would like to read some of my other books they are all available on Amazon. They are stories of genuine animal communication where I have managed to solve problems or helped some way. Some are very emotional, others some really funny misunderstandings. The celebrity book is a world first! It is the first book containing actual celebrity animal readings and thanks to them allowing their personal communication to be published - this has really helped spread the word that animals can psychically communicate with us.

Lastly, thank you for reading about my work and if you needed reassurance that animals do live in spirit, that this book accomplished that.

*****

Reviews are hugely helpful to authors and readers alike. If you truly enjoyed this book, please could you spare me two minutes to put up a review? This helps guide and encourage other people who would maybe like it as much as you did. I would be most grateful. Thank you

*****

 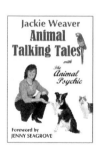 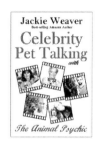

Jackie Weaver
'The Animal Psychic'
www.animalpsychic.co.uk

Printed in Great Britain
by Amazon